Unlocking the Cage

Becoming Authentic

A MEMOIR

Carol Loew

Unlocking the Cage, Becoming Authentic

ISBN: 978-1-7357465-4-8

Library of Congress Cataloging-in-Publication Data is available.

Hawthorne Street Press
P.O. Box 254981
Sacramento, CA 95865

Design by Pamela Dengate

Printed in the United States of America

I dedicate this memoir to
Nancy Grant L.C.S.W.
(of blessed memory)
who unlocked my cage with kindness
and taught me how to be authentic.

CONTENTS

BEGINNING

"Reading is like breathing in;
writing is like breathing out."

Pam Allyn

PROLOGUE

How often have you wondered about yourself?

Wondered how you are perceived by those around you.

You put on what you think is the best face
without having any idea what impression is being made.

As we experience our life passages there is joy, tragedy, simchas (Hebrew for happy occasions) and far too many shiva minyans (Hebrew for Ceremony for the deceased). Have we stopped to enjoy the moments or have we rushed through our busy life and wondered where the years have gone?

I have now reached a respectable old age. No, I will not write it or say it aloud. How did so much time pass and where have I been hiding for so many years?

But no life goes untouched, when you do not pay attention to the red flags that appear before you, the higher spirit (whatever that is for you) will send a big bang. It is important to acknowledge the red flags, the result of a big bang is not a pretty picture.

This is my story. It is complicated but nothing that has not happened to you, either in reality or your mind working overtime. Our religion dictates that we are to do 613 mitzvot (good deeds) in our lifetime. We practice Tikkun Olam, the repair of the world. When you are raised this way, it is so easy to get wrapped up in this purpose and you leave yourself behind.

I am a very spiritual person. I embrace all people and all religions. Interfaith work is my joy. I found I could live each day without me in the picture and I did just that for my adult years. The rewards of my work, wonderful. That something was not right, I had no idea.

Why did I decide stoic and strong was the only emotion I could practice? Why did I hang on to my father when he had a cardiac arrest at the young age of 65, and then being able to give him permission to leave us? Why was my beloved younger brother killed, why was nursing my husband through five years of Cancer a see-saw of emotions. I am filled with "why" and it was the reason for my hiding out doing good work for everyone but me. Does that sound familiar?

In January of 2018, I collapsed from exhaustion. Something called "Self-Care" was not a concept that I practiced or even understood. It was a stunning circumstance, as I had been hiding out for so long, I never thought I would have to come to terms with myself.

Blessed to find a PTSD therapist, a very few caring friends and the plan my higher spirit always had for me, I was given a gift. I had the chance to become acquainted with myself. The authentic me, without being nervous or concerned about whom that person might be. I had been living in and out of a velvety green zippered pea pod to cautiously taste the life of everyone else. My therapist unlocked my self-imposed cage and here I am ready to tell the world that it is okay to be self-caring without being selfish.

I realized that my children only know me as MOM. They have no idea why I am like I am. Their perception is that I am a superwoman and need nothing. They do not know how my childhood affected me as a woman and parent. I made it a point to be the perfect mom for them (impossible). And I maintained that stoic and strong presence for them at all times. They learned early on that I needed nothing and could always take care of every situation. Later in this book, you will find out how they reacted to the new and improved me.

Yesterday, I told my most trusted friend that I was happy. For most of my life, I have been asked "Are you happy?" or "What would make you happy?" I could not even define happiness. The Webster Dictionary defines happy as joyous, pleased and lucky. Today, that is me and I am so "happy" to finally meet me. The authentic me. And the world has not exploded and no one took away my birthday.

Join me on my adventure. You will probably see a bit of yourself here and there. Know that loving others is a joy but loving yourself first will enhance every relationship. Each day will be filled with goodness. When you hit one of those difficult times, you will know that your authenticity will keep you buoyant and back to self-care within a few days.

BEGINNING

"I think writing really helps you heal yourself.

I think if you write long enough,
you will be a healthy person.

That is, if you write what you need to write,
as opposed to what will make money,
or what will make fame."

Alice Walker

BIG GRANDPA AND LITTLE GRANDMA

To make sense of my interesting life, I need to start at the beginning. All four of my grandparents were immigrants. My mother's parents, Molly and Manuel Frucht (pronounced Frook-t) came from Romania. They arrived through Ellis Island and I have no idea how they ended up in California.

Their family consisted of four daughters, born after they arrived in this country. Eldest Charlotte, then Rose, next, my mom Lena. Her name was really Leah but it was spelled wrong in the hospital and their youngest, Gertrude, a late in life unexpected baby. Four daughters was a tough pill to swallow for the macho Manual Frucht, a strong and very controlling man.

"We were teased at school," said my mother, "and called Lotta, Rosie and Lenda Fruit."

Years later, and being very naughty, my cousin, Sylvia, Rose's daughter and I would say when faced with an unpleasant situation "That is really Frucht."

Trust me, many jokes were made about the last name. Nowadays when I am asked by a bank or an account to give my mother's maiden name, I always chuckle as I reply.

Big Grandpa, Manuel Frucht, was an ambitious and determined man. We were taught to honor and obey him. Any questions we might have had about their life before coming to America and why he settled in California was never an allowed discussion.

What I do know is that he was a cattle man in Hollister, California. To quote my mother "Your grandpa would take me to the slaughterhouse with him and make me hold the warm packaged heart in my lap on the ride home."

His next career was as the Jewish milkman in San Francisco. Now that had to be a sight to see, sadly there is not a photograph.

Their final destination was Redwood City, California. Their property was two lots away from the railroad tracks. They had a large property with a home in the center of the lots. A chicken coop and yard, grape arbors, garage and barn combo and many fruit trees. It was quite a lot of fun for grandchildren raised in San Francisco with a very proper upbringing. We could break loose at our grandparent's home. We collected, very carefully as instructed, eggs from the hens, tossed dinner scraps into the chicken yard, planted corn and played among the stalks and never missed waving at an engineer on the passing trains. It was fun.

In Redwood City, Grandpa was the proprietor of the "Main Street Furniture Company, new and used" He had a desk in the front of the store, chairs hanging on nails all around the highest spot on the walls and an assortment of items that he could put out in front of the shop when he opened. In the back right hand corner of the store was an area closed in by tall furniture so there was a place to eat meals. Each day, my grandmother would pack lunch, walk the railroad tracks to take Grandpa his lunch. What a thrill it was for us to walk with her when we visited in the summer. My grandmother, on the other hand, rarely had a happy face. She always looked angry. I guess the daily walk on the tracks was not fun for her.

Every Fourth of July, we would hop into his truck. I will interrupt to add this tidbit, the truck he used to buy the ice that we put into the ice box. He would ask us if we wanted to go to the ice house with him and we would jump into the back of the truck, get the ice and ride back home with it, sitting practically on top of the ice in the heat of the summer. Now, back to July 4th! Grandpa would put all the cousins in the back of the truck, park it on the side of his shop and we watched the parade from the truck. No grandstand ever felt as good. At the same time, Grandma, the aunties and my mom would prepare a feast and serve us in the back of the truck as we watched the Redwood City parade go by. It was such a fun day for the family and I couldn't wait to get back to school and tell my friends all about it.

Another fun time for the cousins was when we were rounded up to pick the fresh fruit. That is fruit, not Frucht. All the older male cousins climbed the trees and placed the apricots into the baskets that the older girl cousins held for them. As I was the youngest and smallest, the boys thought the most fun was to find a rotten apricot and throw it on my head, by mistake, of course! I was always getting my hair washed to get rid of the apricot remains. Today, you can buy apricot shampoo, not my first choice.

After we picked the trees clean, Grandma took us to the back of the chicken coop where she had long tables and we spent our time splitting the apricots, removing the pits, and setting them out in the sun to become dried apricots. Other days, my grandmother would make apricot jam and we would have an entire supply of her extra delicious jam. My favorite to this day.

However, one morning when we were all at the table, I spread some apricot jam on my toast and found an ant in my jam. I shrieked to my elders "Oh no, there is an ant in the jam."

My grandfather asked "Why are you so upset? They taste good and can't eat much of your jam anyway."

To this day, I have an aversion to ever watching anyone eat a bug nor would I ever think it is a luxury."

I have one more very special story about Big Grandpa. He was so methodical. He wore black cotton sleeve covers over his starched dress shirt every single day to work. When he arrived home, he would enter the house, stop and remove his sleeve covers in the laundry area and cleanse his hands in the wash tub. Then head to a shelf over the sink where he would reach for a bottle and shot glass and pour himself a schnapps. Then he was ready to greet the family. We would have dinner and when dinner was over, we would sit entranced by Grandpa. In his usual methodical manner, he would roll his own cigarettes. Very carefully and not drop a speck of tobacco. For Chanukah one year, we found him a pot belly stove ashtray as his gift. That made the after-dinner cigarette even more eventful. He would roll his cigarette, twist the ends, light it and lift the little lid on the ashtray, flick the cigarette ashes into it, close the lid and we would wait for the smoke to come out of the chimney. We were fascinated, Big Grandpa was a giant of a man. A bit scary, but we knew how much he loved all of us.

Little Grandma, on the other hand, was not a happy person. She came from a very aristocratic family in Romania. I believe, or perhaps my mom may have said, that she felt she had married beneath her station in life. She never believed she would be spending her life on a cattle farm, the milkman's wife or walking railroad tracks. While I do not know the real stories of their meeting, marrying and coming to America, I know that she instilled a sense of importance in her daughters that made each of them a diva, with a genuine sense of entitlement. When I get to my parents, there will be much more about my mom and aunties.

One day after school, my parents gathered us in the car and said that we had to head to Redwood City. We had no idea why and since children should be seen and not heard, we were in the dark. Upon arrival, we were ushered into the living room with all our cousins and the door was closed. We heard sobbing from the front of the house but could only speculate on what was going on. Wally, our eldest cousin, was in charge and kept us quiet and well-mannered so we did not bother the adults. Finally, someone came into the room and informed us that Gertrude, the youngest sister had passed away. It was our first experience with death and we were not sure we understood. We realized that Aunt Gertrude always played with us and wasn't like the other adults but she was sweet and kind. For many years into adulthood, especially when having my own children, I asked about her illness and why it caused her death.

Mother said "She was always sickly and different. She suffered from Melancholia."

Now that sounded to me like something from "Little Women" when they had the vapors or something like that. We never had an explanation. I even asked my father but he would not answer either. Obviously, she was born with a disability because it didn't seem that Melancholia, defined as depression, was her problem. That strange day has stayed with me.

My grandparents' home was a gathering place, an adventure and we enjoyed many summer experiences with the family in Redwood City. We stayed with them for several summers before my parents purchased a home in Atherton for our summer home. Each year, we moved to Atherton when our school was out and didn't return home until the week before school began. However, the Main Street Furniture Store, New and Used was still the place to spend Fourth of July and enjoy egg gathering and throwing the leftovers to the chickens.

Manuel Frucht, Molly Blackfield Frucht.
Maternal grandparents.

Frucht Family. Charolotte, Rose,
Lena, Molly & Manual Frucht.
My Mother, Aunts & Grandparents

The entire Frucht Family

LITTLE GRANDPA AND THE WICKED WITCH OF THE WEST

My little Grandpa, Mendel Aizenberg, like my mother's parents, was an immigrant. He arrived at Ellis Island from Poland with his wife, Bessie and their first child, a daughter Bluma.

Years later, when my late husband and I attended Yom Kippur services in Budapest, I noticed that all the men were short, in long overcoats, a hat and looked just like little grandpa.

When they arrived on Ellis Island and were ushered through the long lines, not speaking a word of English, it was so confusing for them. When asked his name he said "Mendel Eisenberg"

The officer asked "How do you spell that?"

Stumbling and nervous he said "Aizenberg" not Eisenberg, the officer phonetically spelled what grandpa said and thus, we became, "How do you spell that?" until I married.

The good news, I always had the front row since my last name started with an A. The bad news, no one could pronounce or spell it. As an aside, when my dad would make a dinner reservation and he was asked his name he always said "Dr. Lloyd." I can't wait to get to the part of my story when the explanation for being Dr. Lloyd makes sense.

Mendel and Bessie had their first son, Martin in 1907, followed by David in 1910 and Sam in 1913. It was during the difficult birth of another baby that my grandmother, Bessie, lost her life in childbirth.

My grandfather Mendel was by trade an embroiderer. He had a small shop on Fillmore Street in the Jewish district of San Francisco. He made gorgeous tallit (prayer shawl) bags, table linens and other personalized items. He created the magnificent bridal veil embellished with love knots for my mother when she married his eldest son, Martin. That wedding veil was preserved and worn at the weddings of all the Aizenberg women. Interesting to note that in 1976, I opened a shop on Burlingame Avenue on the San Francisco Peninsula called "Especially for You." It was a shop of all things personalized. Self- taught, I did all the engraving and personalizing myself. Guess it runs in the bloodlines. When I start to write about myself, I am certain there will be much more about having the courage as a single mom to open a business.

Grandpa found life very difficult trying to raise his children alone. When Mendel and Bessie came from the old country, there were no relatives to help. Grandpa was doing all he could as a widower to tend his business and his family. The bulk of the work was done by Auntie Bluma, so young to have such responsibility. She loved her little brothers and did what was expected of her

Enter the Wicked Witch! Although I don't know any facts, somewhere along the line my grandfather met and married a very unhappy and dour woman. Her name was Ethel (the name fit her) and she was a widow with three sons, Leo, Al and Joe. Imagine blending that family. Again, without having a time frame, this family grew up with the mild mannered quiet little grandpa and the tyrant that didn't like grandpa's children very much and the years passed.

Leo, Ethel's son and my Aunt Bluma fell in love and married. I would have liked to have been a fly on the wall and see that happen. Of course, for the family Cinderella, that was probably her only exposure to men and it made sense at that time. That marriage produced my cousins, Bernard and Annette and as one might have expected that marriage ended in a divorce. Imagine in1940 to be a single mother.

My aunt worked in the famed San Francisco City of Paris department store. At one time, on her limited budget, she lived with her children in an empty store. I thought that was the coolest thing I had ever seen and couldn't wait to go visit and play there. From my 180 degrees lifestyle, at my age, I had no idea what it meant to my aunt and cousins to be living like that. As I got older I realized what their life was all about, it made me very sad. Perhaps that was the beginning of my lifelong desire to practice Tikkun Olam or translated the repair of the world.

But I digress, Ethel's sons and their wives all worked for the Muni Railroad in San Francisco. They were drivers, as well as, loading passengers and collecting fares as people embarked. Often, I would run for a bus and there in front of me was one of the uncles, dressed in the uniform with the little metal coin changer attached to their waist. The bus would drop me at the corner of one of my family's pharmacies and I would go inside for my candy treats and latest comic book before one of our delivery boys would take me home.

My Aunt Bluma was a dear lady and she would always take me to synagogue with her on Saturday, then for lunch and a movie. She had a very unhappy life. However, Bernard was a strong, handsome Marine, went on to Pharmacy school, worked for my dad and changed careers going to Hawaii and teaching at the Punahou School for the duration of his career. He was fun, funny and I adored him. My cousin Annette married a policeman, imagine a Jewish policeman, and they had two sons. Her husband Herb was a wonderful man. On Passover when we ate only matzo, he would entice us with a piece of matzo, buttered, then peanut buttered, jam and topped with sliced banana. I was enthralled and watched each layer after layer being built. To this day, I can't eat a piece of matzo with peanut butter and not think of that wonderful time.

Little grandpa and Ethel had one child together. My dear Auntie Helen. She was a sickly child, bad health followed her throughout her life. She was delicate and beautiful. Similar to the beautiful, slender, pale skinned ladies pictured on sachet boxes and book covers of the era. She was asthmatic and never without her Asthma spray. With great family joy she met a wonderful man, Seymour, who treated her so gently and held her so preciously. Sadly, she passed in her early thirties and left Seymour and our family heartbroken. She was a very special flower.

That is the introduction of Mendel and Bessie's arrival and beginning of life in America for the Eisenberg, oh, excuse me, Aizenberg family.

Bessie & Manuel Aizenberg,
Bluma and Martin

Aunt Bluma (eldest) Grandmother Bessee, May Dad, Martin (2nd), Uncle Sam (youngest, Grandpa Aizenberg with original family, Uncle David (3rd)

Manuel Aizenberg "Little Grandpa", Auntie Helen, Ethel Logasa Aizenberg. Paternal Grandparents & my Father's little sister

"Little Grandpa", with my brother Stephen, outside of Lloyds Pharmacy

PARENTING D -

How does one evaluate parenting? That is an important question. My siblings, Beverly, (of blessed memory) my older sister and Stephen (of blessed memory) my younger brother, have told stories about our family that have caused me to ask the question "Did we grow up in the same home?"

I believe the type of parenting in our home came from two very damaged children raised by immigrants and finding themselves a first generation American with Eastern European culture in their home. In immigrant families, and especially Jewish families, education for their sons was the first priority. I believe both families wanted good lives for their children but their drive to have their sons succeed came before love and affection.

Now, referring back to my previously written grandparent stories, both of my parents struggled with the diversity and conflict in their families. I heard mostly difficult stories and wondered if they ever had fun.

My father, Martin, attended Lowell High School in San Francisco. Lowell High is still the only academic high school in San Francisco. His goal was to be a doctor and he worked in that direction with great determination. However, being the eldest son, when his mother died in childbirth, he had no choice but to take the next best thing to allow him to assist his widowed father and siblings so he transferred to Pharmacy School. This allowed him to graduate sooner but he had to give up his dream.

Martin was a short (Polish trait), round, happy faced and a dear man. His work was his passion and he ran his corner Pharmacy like what we now call Urgent Care facilities. He purchased his pharmacy from Dr. Lloyd and the pharmacy name was Lloyd's Pharmacy. My dad ran his store seven days a week, daily from 10:00 am. to 11:00 pm., Sundays 10:00 am. to 5:00 pm. I would leave for school in the morning while he was still asleep and he came home after we were all in bed. Dinner table conversations like "How was your day?" "What did you learn in school today." just didn't happen.

However, the pharmacy was a haven for us. The candy counter, with the giant box of fudge, was taken for granted. We were also allowed to take comic books home, read them, handle them with care and return them once read for sale to the public. Lloyd's Pharmacy had a soda fountain and that was the best. Shakes, malts, hot fudge sundaes, ice cream cones, all available when desired. That is, if our mom would take us by the store.

If, by chance, we wanted to speak to our father, we had to call him in the store and deal with him that way. If we needed permission to do something, we would be the victim of simply a yes or no depending on how busy he was and if he even heard the request. We never had time to plead our case. Unfortunately, we didn't have a father role model but as is found in most ethnic cultures, the father was held in high esteem and questions about the whys of the situation were unacceptable.

So many things happened in that pharmacy on the corner of Presidio and California. One night my boyfriend and I stopped by the store to say hi and the store was closed. Unheard of!

I went to the gas station, on the opposite side of the street, and asked "Why is my dad's store closed?"

"Oh, you didn't know" uttered the service station attendant. "He was held up, there were gunshots, and I believe he is at the hospital."

I finally reached someone that told me he was at Mt. Zion Hospital and we raced there. I have the vision today of looking down the hall, seeing an older man, sitting stooped over, his head bandaged and I could not believe it would be my father. I ran down the hall and looked at my poor father with his shirt and multicolored necktie soaked in blood. Grateful that he was alive. I cannot say the same for his assistant that handled the soda fountain. Reuben tried and tried to open the cash register, which had jammed in his haste to get it open. The robber thought he was killing time and had sent an alarm and shot him to death. It was the beginning of the end for my dad. It somehow had taken the life out of him. If I had to guess, I would say he had been in the store for 40+ years loving every minute until this tragedy.

Oh, but let's get past the many pharmacy stories and move on to our mother.

I have given you some incite to the Frucht/fruit sisters and my mother was the third girl. Not a favorite birth gender to write about to the relatives in the old country. My grandparents decided to dress my mom up as a boy and send it so that my grandfather would appear more macho to his family. At that time, Jewish families (or perhaps many ethnic families) were blessed with sons and it was a great happiness in the clan. Girls, not so much.

At this point, I would like to quote my difficult mother when she said "Carol, you need to understand that girls are born to serve me but my son is my son."

Thus, in my adult years, I always introduced Stephen this way "Please meet my brother, Steve, who is an only child."

It always got a laugh and I shed another tear inside. I plan to write about my brother, Stephen, at another time. I fell in love with him the day my parents brought him home and that love lives inside me to this day even though he is gone. A sister and brother match that everyone should be blessed to have.

Now, back to Lena. Was she a bad parent? Yes, I think she was. Did she do it knowingly? I don't think so. I believe she was severely damaged as a child. After all, being dressed as a boy had to start a path to feeling a lack of confidence. I heard many stories during the years about her unpleasant childhood and the cruelty of the sisters with each other.

My father told me, when I was an adult, "both sides of the family have bad female interactions and it has been going on for years."

My mother's idea of raising children was to abuse and punish them because it builds character. I guess I need to say that I am the biggest character in my family!

My grandparents, having four daughters, did not feel the pressure to encourage them to higher education. They were groomed to be good Jewish housewives and were prepared for marriage, not for taking care of themselves. Having difficult role models, they did not appear to marry for love.

My father had a person in his life that he loved dearly. Her father was very comfortable with my father.

One night he said to my dad “Marty, you are a very good man and when you marry my daughter, I am going to give you an up-to-date pharmacy of your very own”.

My dad being a proud, self-made man, walked out of the house, went home, slammed the door to his room and stayed there for two days, my aunt told me. He was insulted and broke up with Dorothy.

Soon after, Martin met Lena. My mother was a very nervous and frail woman.

She was the helpless type and always struggled. In my father’s state of mind, he needed to be needed and my mother was right there and available. Little did he know at the time that Lena had a mean streak and sense of entitlement that would be the downfall of a happy family in the future.

Many years later, I asked him if he had the same choice to make over again, would he do the same thing?

His answer “Cookie, you bet I would have taken the offer.”

You can see, my parents’ marriage was not made in heaven. It was not a loving home. On the outside looking in, one could say we were the “perfect” Jewish family. The right house, schools, clothing, social arena, friendships and on and on. What was missing was a safe and loving place to be.

Were my parents good or bad parents? I didn’t have role models, so how would I know???? At least, I didn’t give them an F for parenting.

My parents, Martin Aizenberg and Lena Frucht Aizenberg in the corn field at the Frucht Farm. They seemed Happy!

Mother with her daughters caught by a street photographer in Downtown San Francisco

Lena with Bev, Carol and Stephen, Does she seem happy?

Sunday Brunch at the Aizenbergs in San Francisco. My dad was actually home.

NOT THAT UNCLE SAM

It is time to share life with Uncle Sam. Every Jewish family has an Uncle Sam or "Samala" as the old country folks called him.

Uncle Sam moved into our family home when I was three. He was my father's youngest brother. Uncle Sam was a jovial man but inside I think he was sad. It was a safe place for him to live with his big brother. My father watched over him as he grew up and made sure he was educated. Uncle Sam followed my father into Pharmacy school and soon joined the family business.

Our three stores were in the Richmond District of San Francisco. Dad's store at Presidio and California Streets and Uncle Sam was at 6th Avenue and California Street. We later had a store midway between our locations on California Street. Perhaps, we can consider our business one of the first pharmacy chains!

What fun it was as children to have our own world of fun. From the candy case, a soda fountain and comic books, we were constantly entertained. A funny thing about our stores, we had a special phone hook up. I guess it would be classified as an intercom system. It was a square black box with a hand crank on the side….no, it was not a pencil sharpener! It was one ring for Lloyd's pharmacy, two rings for Park Presidio Pharmacy and three for Laurel Village. I still laugh when I think about it.

Later on, when I was living in San Francisco as a single mother of two, I worked for a medical office half a block from our Laurel Village store. Our medical office had many patients that had their prescriptions filled with "Dr. Lloyd" and were on their way to my dad's store. Often, I would send him treats with a love note. The most notable of these, when our patient that owned a Jewish deli brought me a plate of kosher green-tinted corned beef with cabbage on St. Patrick's Day, I sent it to my dad with another patient on their way to have a Rx filled. It was fun while it lasted. Seems like I was always working across the street from my dad.

Back to my uncle. Uncle Sam played many roles for me. Uncle, Godfather and he became my stepfather later in our lives. He had one great love in his life and when that broke up, he decided marriage was not for him. He was always a stand in for my dad, if you remember an earlier story about my dad's work hours. Uncle Sam was home for dinner. Often, he would take us to the boardwalk of the San Francisco beach, park the car and get us an ice cream.

He would say, "Let's stay parked here awhile and watch the funny people."

The beachfront was amazing. Stand after stand of goodies. A huge Merry-go-Round, arcade games and "Laughing Sal," a giant puppet in a glass window that rocked back and forth laughing all the time. She was dressed in bright clothing and had a smile on her face but she was still very scary to me.

Uncle Sam was a confirmed bachelor. He was such a people person. Always chatting away in his store and never tired of telling stories.

My sibs and I had them numbered and would say, "Oh no, not #78 again!"

He called me the "Little Songbird" and each year gave me a birthday card with a songbird on it. It felt special that he picked that card just for me. I still have them.

Right in front of his drug store was the bus transfer spot when I was heading home from Lowell High School. I always checked in the store to see if there was a delivery boy present to run me home instead of the bus. Our delivery boys picked us up on rainy days, drove me to dance lessons and I believe they disliked every minute of driving the boss's kids around instead of delivering orders and getting tips!!!!

Uncle Sam was a past master of his Masonic Lodge and a Shriner. His lodge was his life. He had a gang of friends that he traveled with and invited to our home for a weekly poker game. From his travels, he always sent great postcards from his destination spot and returned with fantastic gifts for us. We were certainly considered his kids since he was home with us most of the time and he had to deal with all our day-to-day issues.

April 25,1944 was a banner day in Uncle Sam's life. That was the day my dear brother, Stephen, was born. You would have thought Uncle Sam was his father, the joy that he had at this birth. (Hmmm, does make one stop to wonder) They were buddies from the get-go and as Steve grew up, they had adjoining rooms in our home with a bathroom in between. After Stephen arrived, our family description became Stephen and the girls. Even our Princess Beverly lost some of her luster with our three adults. I adored my brother and began to enjoy my middle status, after all, what is the best part of a sandwich?

My father, dedicated to his store and having interests elsewhere, got very comfortable with Uncle Sam filling in for him as the father figure. Our picture-perfect family continued the dysfunction in the usual manner. Mother was a tyrant, Daddy an absentee father and Uncle Sam as the buffer. Listening to our whining and trying to smooth over any issues usually without much success. Still, he was there to listen.

In 1977, my father passed away at just 69 years old. He arrived home from the store, walked up the stairs and said he was not feeling well. Uncle Sam and mother took him to Mt. Zion Hospital emergency room. A nurse put him flat on an examination table, filling his lungs with fluid and he had a cardiac arrest. He lingered for eleven days and quietly passed away. During his coma, he stopped breathing and someone told me to go into him and make him breathe. I wrapped him in my arms and rubbed his diaphragm encouraging him to breathe. A nurse was in the room with me and I suddenly heard her gasp.

"He is breathing," she uttered, "I can't believe it."

I was stunned and walked out of his room in shock. What had I done? Did I stop him from the path he had chosen to take? Filled with anxiety, I ran to my Rabbi's office and asked him what I did. He advised me that I held on to my father and he would not leave us until I gave him permission. The next day when I arrived at the hospital, I went into his room, held him and told him that all would be well and if he and G_d decided it was his time, to leave us when he felt ready. The next morning, I received a phone call that he had passed. It was haunting for me.

Several years later, Mother and Uncle Sam decided to sell the big home and move to Sacramento to be closer to my brother (You know, the "only child") leaving my sister and me to be the only family left in the Bay Area

Maybe five or so years later, I was living in beautiful Burlingame on the San Francisco Peninsula, with my two sons, busy getting ready to go to my shop. I was in the shower, when my son yelled, "Telephone, Mom."

I yelled back, "Can't you see I am in the shower. I will call whoever it is back."

"No, Mom, it is Uncle Steve and he needs to talk with you right now."

Frightened to hear that and wondering what awful news he was going to tell me, I jumped out of the shower, threw on a robe, my hair dripping everywhere and I grabbed the phone.

"Quick, I hate bad news," I said, decibels above my normal voice.

"No, no," he exclaimed. "You have to be in Reno tomorrow."

"Not me," I said, "It is the weekend before Father's Day and it is an important time for me to be in my gift shop."

I owned my own shop called "Especially for You." All personalized gifts and I did the monogramming, imprinting and engraving. How absurd to think I could take time away from the business at such a lucrative gift buying time.

"Carol", he said, very agitated by this time. Mom and Uncle Sam are getting married tomorrow afternoon. I have arranged for a Rabbi and a hotel. You and Bev have to get together and get to Reno tomorrow. You will be home by evening."

So shocked I said, "Okay. I will make it happen."

I called my sister and got really into the spirit. I ran to the store, imprinted some cocktail napkins, ordered wine glasses asap and engraved a wedding cake knife. Beverly's assignment was to find a pretty nightgown and robe. We called Reno and ordered flowers and a small wedding cake. I figured if we were having a wedding, we would make it a real celebration. The next morning, we met and raced to Reno.

We gathered and took Mom to our room to get her ready. Steve took Uncle Sam to get ready in his suite. Then to the Rabbi's chapel, a wedding ceremony and back to the hotel for a celebration. Champagne, food, wedding cake. Much excitement! Uncle Sam gave each of us a gold coin to commemorate the occasion. He was an avid coin and stamp collector.

Mother gave each of us girls one of her rings. Bev received a diamond owl so that she would always be wise, my sister-in-law, Lenore, was given a diamond four leaf clover so she would always be lucky and I received her tenth anniversary ring, a bridge of diamonds, five on each side. I wish I could say that the "gift" was sentimental but it held very bad memories for me. Perhaps I can find somewhere in my writing to include that episode. Anyway, we had breakfast together and by late afternoon, I was back in my shop.

What made them get married? They were working on their trust when their attorney decided to throw out a funny statement.

He said, "Too bad you aren't married. Since you both have the same last name, it would make the paperwork easier."

I guess that had an impact on Uncle Sam. Was it a forever love from a distance or a cost saving action? That is the question? I can only speculate that their affection for each other had to exist for many years. Later that same week after seeing their attorney, mother was resting and Uncle Sam was doing some household chores. He went up to her, got down on one knee and proposed to her. Imagine, power of suggestion and a first marriage in his sixties.

My lesson learned from that occasion, always remember that within 24 hours, your life can completely turn around. I was engraving gifts one day, in Reno the next day and back to engraving gifts by evening of the same day.

As Uncle Sam was approaching his 80th birthday, he was struggling with many health problems, mostly heart related. We had several false alarms and rushed to Sacramento but he managed to fight his way back. However, the call came that was the last one. He was in the hospital and I needed to get there fast. I dropped everything and got on the road.

Uncle Sam had asked me to keep his life going, no matter what had to be done. I went to the hospital and while going to his room, I heard over the loudspeaker that there was a code blue. As I approached his room, there was the team working on him. I was the only family member present at the time. His heart doctor walked out of the room and asked me what he should do? I couldn't find my voice since I felt that I wanted to let him go and be at peace. All I could think about was my brother accusing me of giving consent against Uncle Sam's wishes.

Suddenly, I heard the doctor's voice, practically yelling at me, "Carol, what do you want me to do?"

I answered him, "Do whatever you must to keep him going. That was his request."

Several days later, we all gathered in his room, knowing it was close to the end. It is so difficult to stand by and wait for someone to pass. I could only pray that G_d had a plan for him. My mother was exhausted and Steve decided to take her home for a break. Beverly left the room and was in the hall. I sat down with Uncle Sam, held his hand and told him what a wonderful uncle and dad he was.

He looked at me and said, "Om" (whatever that meant) seven times.

I assumed he was trying to ask me to handle things for him. I know he thought he was talking in sentences.

With each om, I said, "I will take care of it, yes, I understand."

At some point, I felt a hand on my back and Beverly said, "Carol, he is gone."

She had been at the nurse's desk and the nurse informed my sister that his monitor indicated that he had passed. I just put my head on his chest and thanked the higher spirit for putting him at peace.

Uncle Sam enjoyed a good life. He took advantage of any opportunity that came his way. He liked his customers, mixing medicines, going to lodge, making bets on the horses and many other things. He was not complicated but took life as it came.

He was the glue that held us together with his acceptance of each day. Like an ocean liner, he kept us on an even keel. He was a good man.

Uncle Sam -
How cute is
this picture?

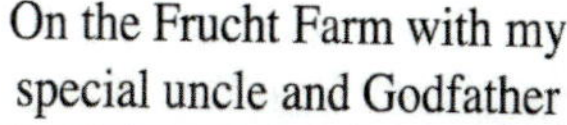
On the Frucht Farm with my special uncle and Godfather

"Good Afternoon, Park Presidio Pharmacy" said the corner Pharmacist

Uncle Sam the proud master of his Masonic Lodge. Soon to be Shriner and recipient of a 50 year cap for his membership and dedication

Lena & Sam marry in Las Vegas

At the wedding reception, we all had a wonderful reason to celebrate Uncle Sam was now our step dad too!

THE MIDDLE CHILD

Just to bring you up to date, as of March, 30 2022, I am now an only child. You will learn about my life as one of three siblings, an older sister and a younger brother. Their stories, as my siblings, will follow throughout with many memories of shared time. Most of all, with love.

I have discovered that I love to see the written word. Suddenly, my curiosity to review my life has become very important. To leave my history to my children has replaced what I thought was my mission in life. Thinking my journey was to save the world (Hebrew: Tikkun Olam), lately I have learned that saving myself was the true mission. For other middle children, female or male, this manuscript describes the lessons I have learned in my life so far.

When I tried to learn my family "truths" as I grew older, my dear Uncle Sam, who was my uncle, step-father and G_d father, said "Cookie, what is the matter with you? What are you talking about and trying to do?"

I pleaded, "What were things like when I was a baby, were my parents happy to have me? Did they hold me? Was I loved?"

I could see his discomfort and made an excuse to go to my room. He only peaked my concerns and scared me so I tucked it away and went back to my quiet, secret place in that green pea pod.

My siblings were born at Mt. Zion Hospital in San Francisco, California. My older sister, Beverly, on 01/01/1935 (but more about that later) and my younger brother Stephen (of blessed memory) on 04/25/1944. I, however, was born in Dante Sanatorium at Broadway and Van Ness in San Francisco. A splendid piece of architecture. All taupe brick with ornate trim taking most of a San Francisco block. I later learned it was a mental hospital.

Why was it different from the other births? Through the years, we often passed Dante Hospital. I always asked why I was born there and I was told it was a private hospital and I had very special treatment. I wish I knew the truth. It didn't make sense to me. I can only imagine, but I still do not know why, my birth was in another hospital. Perhaps my mother suffered some type of depression. It is a question that will never be answered.

A family tradition established when Beverly was born has been our bassinet. I do not know how it came to our family but Beverly was the first to use it. It has been redecorated for new arrivals for generations. All of us used it for our babies and the next generation has used it for their new arrivals. It is 2022 and Beverly's first great-grandchild, a boy named Jack, is enjoying his first six months in the "Aizenberg" antique bassinet.

With so few memories of my first five years, I can still recall my favorite nanny. She was a charming French woman who truly felt like a grandmother, thus our permission to address her as Grandmere. She taught us how to embroider, knit and crochet. She was with us every day and left after our dinner and bath-time. Being a problem eater my entire life, Grandmere made my favorite dish that has stayed with me to this day: Potato Omelet. I can smell the delicious aroma from the frying pan of the sliced potatoes being sauteed, an egg base and cheese added to pull it all together. Even the taste is still familiar with the cheese-soaked slices of potato but not overdone. Too bad I was so young and not interested in learning how to make it myself. Every attempt has been a disaster!

My spot as the second girl, as well as being the middle child has been a genuine see-saw of an experience. Not having to break barriers as the first born or try new things, nor being the baby in the family given so much extra attention that you feel suffocated at times, I was able to twist and turn without being noticed very much. Isn't that the royal family refers to as the Heir and the Spare? Being the "spare" has its advantages. I wanted to believe that with Uncle Sam it would be one adult for each child. Not so! Mother adored Stephen, my father adored Beverly and Uncle Sam was smitten with Steve from the day he was born. Seems I lost out in the adult affection lottery, but then I have always said that I wouldn't want to have me as a child or a sibling. Too precocious, outspoken and a bit of a smart aleck. To this day, trying to keep me quiet is a real task.

I am, however, blessed with my birth order since I could be on my own most of the time. I learned to balance my successful endeavors with my never-ending failures. Best way to learn your lessons: having to get in and out of problems on your own. Lessons you never forget.

Truth be told, it is wonderful to have siblings. Of course, you often disagree, have days go by when you are so angry at them you stop speaking, slam doors, shed tears and feel like you will never be friends again. Then there are times when you can truly enjoy vacations together, planning events together and more. Why? Because from day one, you are family and learn to do everything the same way. There is no one more familiar, understanding, loyal, supportive and able to finish your sentences than your sibling. No matter how different you are, when push comes to shove, you are always there for each other.

Not a day goes by that I do not give thanks for Beverly and Stephen. They were my book ends and my safe place. There is not a single happy or sad event that didn't bring us together in a loving embrace, even if we had not been communicating for ages. Losing a sibling is like losing a body part, totally irreplaceable. Family is everything.

No! A second girl! Now we have the spare but need the heir!

"Don't you take my picture" I said to the photographer

"I am so happy to be visiting my dad at Lloyd's Pharmacy behind the soda fountain

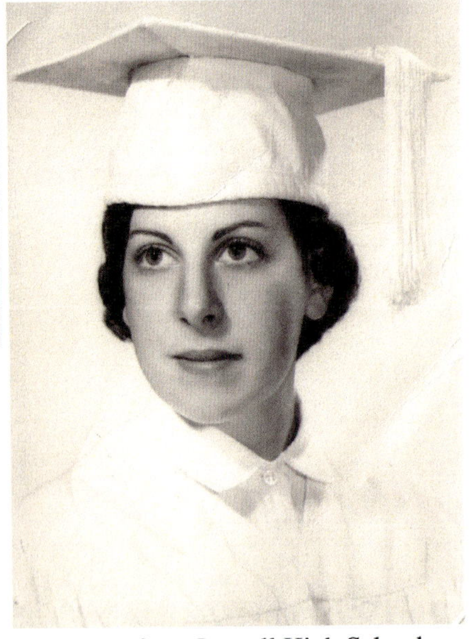

Graduation from Lowell High School in San Francisco. So many memories!

A GEM FOR A SISTER

My sister's name is Beverly Pearl. The eldest daughter of Martin and Lena, she was a blessing and they called her their princess. Why? Because on January 1, 1935, she was the only girl born in San Francisco, California. All the rest were boys.

It was five years before my parents decided to start their family. While tradition dictates that having a boy first is perfection, Lena and Martin were thrilled with their beautiful baby girl. Although I did not arrive for several years after, I understood that Beverly was the perfect child.

Beverly was beautiful and remains a gorgeous woman to this day. She was sweet, polite, obedient and a source of great pride for the family. My parents decided to start a tradition and had an open house every New Year Day for as long as I can remember. The sideboard in their dining room held a large sheet cake reading "Happy (fill in the age) Birthday to our Princess. That wasn't always an easy pill to swallow since I was a summer baby and not the best time for a party. Everyone was always on vacation.

Beverly had a gorgeous voice. She took voice lessons and often appeared in light opera productions. We took dancing lessons but we seemed to divide the talent with Bev being the voice and me, the hoofer! I couldn't carry a note or so I thought.

Naturally, Beverly was pursued by many young men. She was always the prettiest girl in the room, only surpassed by her gentle, polite and loving manner. She was loved and adored by many. To this day, she can hardly tell a story of her past without mentioning the heartbroken boyfriends that were madly in love with her. She really had the "pick of the litter."

Somehow, my mother always made me aware that I was the "spare" and pondered why I couldn't do things like Beverly. It didn't do a lot to cement our relationship but then, my mother was simply playing out the unhappiness she had with her two sisters.

Bev and I shared a bedroom for many years. We had a magnificent Victorian bedroom set that, believe it or not, I still have in my master bedroom. Yes, it carries many memories but it makes me feel happy when I walk into my room.

Recently, when I was sharing a memoir story with Beverly, she asked eagerly, "Did you write about our sharing a bed?"

Of course, I hadn't but memories floated about my head and I realized how many memories I had of life with my beautiful sister.

At one point in our young lives, Beverly caught Scarlet Fever. What is Scarlet Fever, you may wonder? All I recall is that our home had a quarantine sign posted on it and we were forced to stay inside. It is 2022, sound familiar only without a sign? Our home, at the time, had glass doors dividing the rooms. There were eight glass panels. While Bev was quarantined, she and I would sit on each side of the door and, through the glass, chatter and play games. It was fun to have a sister of my own.

The most exciting part of our childhood was our theatrical involvement. You will be reading more about my dancing story but the story of our youth is our show biz time as the "Gay Sisters." Of course, that was years ago and we used my middle name of Gay as our stage name. Stanley Kahn, our dance coach was our dance teacher. He decided to have us perform a dance number he choreographed called "Me and My Shadow." At the time, there was a famous entertainer, Ted Lewis, that actually had as his hallmark, the (real) "Me and My Shadow."

Bev's generosity and warmth made her the perfect grandmother, friend and sister. At one time, we both ran clothing stores with the same company. Her shop was in Fremont and mine in Alameda. We would both go home on the Dumbarton bridge to access the Peninsula more easily. All the toll takers knew us and would give us a heads up on which of us was first or mention that my sister already passed by. As single moms, we would take group trips with our children and have a fabulous time. My children learned to swim in her pool in San Mateo. So many happy memories.

Several years ago, Beverly moved to Sacramento to be closer to family. Being closer to family has been good for Bev, although her health has not been as good as one hoped. She is living in a wonderful independent living place near her children. To add to the interest of this situation, her ex, the children's father, is living in the same place.

Beverly remains today a lovely woman. She has that beautiful smile that endears her to most people. Her residence is filled with many wonderful people and lots of activity. Dialysis occupies three days of her week for a long period of time, but she still is enjoying life. Her latest blessing is becoming a great-grandmother with the birth of Jack, the son of Mitchell's eldest daughter, Sarah and her husband Jaime. Mitchell's youngest daughter, Shelby and her husband David, will make Beverly a great-grandmother for the second time in April.

Beauty begets beauty and Beverly has been blessed with a wonderful life. She has been precious as a pearl, her perfect middle name.

Note: *Beverly passed away January 24, 2023.*

Sisters

Trying to recreate
"Me & My Shadow"
at my folks party!

Sisters Celebrate

A PIECE OF MY HEART BROKEN FOREVER

From the day Stephen was brought home from the hospital until the day he was buried in 2014, I adored him. No matter the circumstances, the good times and the bad, my heart was filled with love for him.

April 25,1944 was a special day for everyone in our family. My precious brother, Stephen, appeared on the scene. If you remember past chapters, you will recall that Uncle Sam was already living with us and we had three parents. One for each child, no way.

My mom's world came together when she had Stephen. Although she called him her war casualty (she had a way of insulting and making it sound acceptable) she spent every minute fussing over him. She sent him to school on his first day in white pants, a white shirt and plaid jacket with the collar of the shirt outside of his coat collar, carrying a bouquet of flowers in his hand. I don't have to tell you how that went over with his classmates but I felt badly for him. When I tried to explain it to Mother, you can just guess what response I was given!

In spite of it, Steve was an intelligent, overachiever and attained much success. As an adult, his closest companion became a vodka bottle. It was strange for our family as we did not have alcohol issues within our family. He was a controlled drinker, only at night, but his mood swings were abrupt and angry. I still felt the warm spot in my heart, even when his rage was directed to me.

One confrontation we had was when he was still a teenager. I was divorced and living back in San Francisco with my sons. He was at my home and did something (who remembers what?) that was totally unacceptable. I was so angry at him and asked him to leave my home. I was devastated that I had a serious falling out with him. I was hurting all day. That night when I got home, finished dinner and put the boys to bed, I was painfully exhausted.

As I got ready to go to bed, I turned down the bedspread and there before my eyes was a box of See's candy with a card. Steve was perhaps

13 but he apologized on his card and gave me the box of candy. I was moved to tears and could not love him anymore than I did at that moment. Although his exterior was that of a shark, his heart was truly golden.

Steve married, had two children and moved to Sacramento as a banker. He moved on from that job and became one of the most successful developers in the Sacramento area.

A side fact of the situation is that our parents, Steve's in-laws and my first husband's parents all lived on the same street in San Francisco. They were all friends! You can imagine the lively visits on Encanto Way and the invisible darts that circulated when both Steve and I divorced their children, our spouses.

Life moved on, Steve remarried, had two more children and moved to Las Vegas in the path of progress. He never missed the chance to buy any property that caught his eye. He was the owner of the Las Vegas News helicopter plus two other helicopters and acquired bigger and better toys.

He built a large private school which he planned to be his retirement annuity. I was a greeter at the school opening and it had everything. He then went on to build a Conservative Synagogue which he called his gift to G-d, expressing his gratitude for a good life.

When the recession hit, Steve was the last of the current crop of developers that lost their footing. He thought he had insulated his business and it couldn't happen to him. His school was to be his annuity for the future, but that was the first to go. Then their magnificent home in a gated community, embellished with every possible amenity—complete with an elevator so my parents could visit and not have to climb stairs. Shelley, his current wife, decorated with every detail down to the last ruffle. It was unimaginable that the high was so high. And the soon to be low, so devastating.

As his world was falling apart, his marriage also crumbled. Steve always purchased one of the homes in each of his developments from his first project forward. It was not a pleasant break up and not one that Steve expected. He was truly broken to learn that all of those he helped, and many he started on the path of success, no longer knew him. He put on a great facade for everyone while he was trying to keep all the pieces together. He was fighting a losing battle.

Steve had purchased a property in Leeds, Utah when times were good. It was a large horse property on a cul-de-sac with one other estate. It was his dream property and said it would be his retirement place. Although I never saw the property, it was described as having a magnificent main house, a delightful guest house, eternity pool, horse area, place for a drag strip for the boy's race cars and unlimited landscaped grounds. I was not happy when he purchased property in Utah as it was a place I visited and determined I would never visit again. No matter how many times he asked, I always had an excuse. He had the entire basement floor of the main house filled with all my parent"s belongings. He begged me to come and help him sort through it all. Even that couldn't get me there. After his death, there was a broken water pipe in the house and all the contents of the basement ended up water soaked and had to be disposed of. Pictures, family treasures and much more lost along with him. Perhaps we lost many memories but things are replaceable. My best friend and brother could never be replaced. I miss him every day.

Besides the horses, I understand the boys had dirt bikes, raced cars and had nothing but fun in the Leeds house. When the split took place, Steve only wanted to have the Leeds property. He gave Shelley everything else so that the boys would always be taken care of. He moved to one of his rental homes in Vegas with his beloved furry friends, Happie and Pixie. They are what kept him alive and moving forward.

Steve traveled back and forth from Sacramento in a beautiful motorhome with his dogs. He spent about three months with us at the RV Park at Cal Expo. His eldest son, Mark, daughter-in-law, Debbie, and their children reside here. He was such a proud grandfather, holding his grandson in his arms as he went through the ritual ceremony of B'rit Malit (Circumcision for Jewish male children). Who knew that he would not live to see his daughter give birth to twins, a boy and a girl?

Steve had a lovely girlfriend, Jan. She was gentle, easy going, low maintenance and just the right person for Steve at this transition. She had no interest in material things and believed that the sun rose and set because of him. She and I became very close since we both loved this man. To this day, we consider ourselves sisters.

Their relationship was calm, easy going and it was so much fun to be with them. Of course, loving my brother, whatever was good for him was good for me.

On Thursday, July 17, 2014, I had what I thought was a normal day. The day ended when I chatted with my sister in Tiburon, then I went to sleep. However, I tossed and turned all night like I had three cups of coffee before bed. I guess I fell asleep around 5 or 6 a.m. I awoke early the next morning, went downstairs to make a cup of coffee when the phone rang. I looked at the caller ID and it was my sister!

I picked up the phone and said, "I just spoke to you last night. What did you forget to tell me?"

"Carol, please go and sit down," was her somber reply.

"What did you say?" I answered. At that point, I started to walk upstairs where my husband was getting ready to go to his cancer radiation treatment.

"Please, Carol, sit down. I am going to tell you the worst news ever."

"What are you going to tell me?"

She replied, "Stephen is dead."

"Stephen who?" I asked, not even thinking it could be our Stephen.

"Stephen, our brother," she said.

With that I handed the phone to Harry and hoped he would make sense of it. As for me, I felt like a white, round metal container slammed down over my brain and I was a walking zombie.

Then the nightmare really began. The story is heartbreaking. My brother was killed by a FORMER (note: not a retired) policeman. Steve was not a permanent resident of the small community but he did know that an elderly couple occupied the other estate in the cul-de-sac. Steve knew that the husband of the home had a stroke and was in the hospital. His elderly wife was at home, he assumed alone. He appeared to have heard gunshots. There were no witnesses but the dogs. Jan was not in Leeds with Steve, she always joined him at the end of her work week Friday evening.

Steve's property was surrounded by security cameras and this is what my nephew saw on film: Steve fed his dogs, ate his first dinner course, put his entree in the microwave and took the dogs out for a final time after their meal. The camera continues with Steve, sitting on the diving board watching the pups and suddenly jumping up, grabbing the dogs, racing into the house and coming out with a handgun (registered to him) by his side. He was dressed in khaki shorts, a yellow tank top, no shoes and he had a head of gorgeous gray hair.

What we found out later was that one shot killed him on the edge of his property. It seems the couple in the other house had two daughters. One a flight nurse, the other the administrative assistant to the most prominent criminal lawyer in Salt Lake City. Her husband, the former cop, had a shooting range, sold guns and had a gun blog talking about killing. Of course, immediately taken down from social media.

At 1 a.m. on July 18, my 14-year-old nephew's phone rang. He answered and a voice said, "Do you know Stephen Aizenberg?"

"Yes," replied my nephew, Sam. "He is my father."

"Is your mother available?" asked the voice at the other end of the phone.

"I will get her," said Sam, confused and nervous by the strange call late at night.

Shelley took the phone and was informed that Stephen had been shot and killed in Leeds. I have no knowledge of what happened then except that Shelley called a policeman friend of the family thinking it was a prank. Sadly, it was a fact.

Meanwhile, Jan was called. She raced the entire two hours to get to Leeds, screaming in disbelief all the way. She was also terrified for the dogs and she couldn't wait to get there. When she arrived, the dogs had been taken to a shelter. The following days were filled with confusion and sadness.

As is my usual characteristic, I remained stoic and strong. I spoke at each of the shiva minyans (traditional Jewish ceremony after burial. Family and friends gather at sunset each night for up to seven nights). I spoke about the blessing that I wished for everyone: That they should experience such a deep love that never changed. I also described the last three years of talking or emailing every day with Stephen, with a sign off of "Love you and miss you." I also explained how grateful I was for the gift of his evolving business that allowed us to share such a close and meaningful relationship, one that could not have happened if the business climate had stayed the same. What a blessing that we shared it all in those last three years.

A lasting memory of when Stephen was still alive and visiting here, I was driving over the Howe Avenue bridge going downtown. Halfway across I heard a horn honking at me. I looked to my left and driving right next to me was my brother. He was headed to Home Depot. We laughed and waved like we had just won the lottery. Since he did not live full-time in Sacramento, seeing him driving next to me was just terrific. I touch my window each time I drive by that spot, tears fill my eyes, and I gaze at the sky and hope he is watching over me.

Each day I am grateful that I was gifted with his love and sharing for the last three years of his life. Like all of us, he was human, flawed, up, down, happy, angry—but no matter what the mood or situation, I had the joy of having him part of my life. I miss him every day. He owns a special spot in my heart.

What a gift my brother was to me.
We had a special friendship

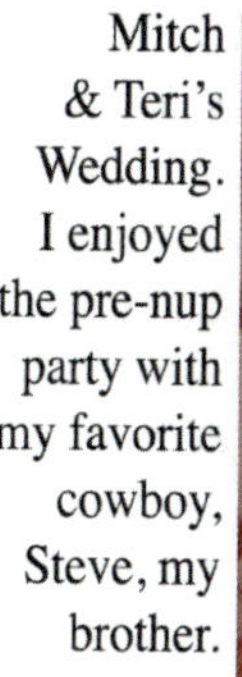

Mitch & Teri's Wedding. I enjoyed the pre-nup party with my favorite cowboy, Steve, my brother.

Always best friends

What a loss! We were attached at the hip - I adored him!

Steve's Surprise Birthday Party

GOODBYE GOLDIE

My mother, possessed of delusions of grandeur, insisted that my sister and I were perfectly accomplished young ladies. Young meaning maybe five and seven years old. What a road we traveled to satisfy her unfulfilled youthful desires.

For starters, Mother had home tutors for her dear daughters. A dance teacher and an elocution coach came to our home for lessons. She insisted that dance training would give us good posture, poise and grace and our diction would be enhanced by Elocution lessons.

Then she hired a French nanny to teach us to knit, crochet and, perhaps, learn a little bit of the French language. We loved our Grandmere as she was with us daily through dinner and we truly loved her for her sweet and gentle ways.

Our elocution lessons were something else. We sat with our teacher, I cannot even remember her name or what she looked like but I can remember one of her delightful (and I use the term loosely) poems for me to recite. Beverly's recitations were a bit more grown up. Here is what I had to learn; funny, I still remember it!

"Little fly upon the wall
Don't you have no clothes at all
Gee, you must be cold."

Wonder how much my mother paid to have me learn how to recite something so silly. Oh, there were many more to come and, for the life of me, I understand I still have a San Francisco accent and speak too softly. I have even been told I mumble. Diction, perfect, people trying to hear it, not so good.

Our dance teachers were a duo named the Wyatt sisters. I can't imagine where in the world my mother found them since they looked like relics from another era. The sisters came to our home each week and we had our dancing lesson in the living room. Little did my mother realize that I thought dancing was the end all, be all. Of course, as always, I kept that secret in my cocoon and just followed directions.

After a bit of time, I danced with such exuberance that I kicked the side table over and that was the sad end of our poor goldfish Goldie. She didn't know what hit her. Mother's patience was stretched after that misfortune but she always found me to be an impossible child even before I killed Goldie.

As I became interested in having more advanced dance training, mother agreed to sign us up to attend the Mason-Kahn Dance Studio. Pat Mason was a Ballet teacher and Stanley Kahn was a choreographer and Dance Director for the Shipstad & Johnson Ice Follies. I absolutely believe that it was my mother's dream to have a movie star in her family but it certainly was not on my father's radar!

I must share the funniest story about Miss Wyatt. She gave us each a dance bag made from woven fabric and mine was orange and brown, I don't much like that combination. It was my dance bag and I tolerated it.

I have no idea what excuse my mother gave the sisters for not giving us lessons anymore but we certainly had an embarrassing incident after we stopped our lessons.

One day, soon after switching to Mason-Kahn Studio, Bev and I were on the bus going to dance class. The bus made a stop to pick up passengers and guess who got on that very bus. Right, it was the Wyatt sisters. Quickly, Bev and I hid our dance bags behind our backs and made respectful conversation with our former teachers. Luck was on our side when they departed the bus before our stop.

By that time, I was the dancing queen and I had found my happy place. My destination was to Broadway to choreograph the hit of the year. What a path I led in my world of theater until it came crashing down. We never get do-overs on our lost dreams but how I wish I knew then what I discovered on my path to authenticity.

JUNIOR HIGH JINX

San Francisco is such a beautiful city. To quote the late, great Herb Caen (San Francisco columnist that wrote about the character and characters of the city), coined the city "Baghdad by the Bay." Driving through San Francisco is a sightseeing tour of magnificent architecture, one building more beautiful than the other. Or am I seeing it only through the eyes of a native of the city?

My school was Presidio Junior High School. It was located in the "Avenues" of the Richmond District. A stunning brick building taking up an entire city block, it had a wonderful auditorium for those of us that thrived on theater arts. We all felt so grown up with our multiple classes, electives and the sense that we knew we were not in grammar school anymore.

Always wanting to volunteer for something, I became a door monitor. It was my job to make sure that students stayed on campus and did not wander off during the school day. How important I felt!! Little did I know that the privilege would be violated by none other than me.

I had a tremendous crush on one of my schoolmates named Kenny Crook. He had a girlfriend whose name was Annie and I was very jealous. However, every time Kenny walked by me, he would smile and say "Hello." I thought I would faint.

So many years have passed and I can't quite remember the perfect sequence of how my crush became special. I like to look back and think that magically he broke up with Annie and was available but I can't swear to it. All I know is that I had my first bad case of puppy love.

My assigned space as a door monitor was the doors that led into the auditorium area. Not a heavily traveled walkway. For some reason, Kenny always passed that way to go back to class.

He would stop and say "Hi Carol. How are you today? Much traffic?"

I would blush and say some dumb thing like "I didn't really count."

Pretty silly! Soon, our conversations were longer, we would see each other between classes and the friendship was moving forward.

One beautiful sunny and warm day (seldom seen in the city by the Bay) led us astray and we decided to leave campus, go for a walk and then return to school. It was so romantic. The area of San Francisco, known as Sea Cliff, was magnificent. The estates reminded one of a movie set. We strolled over the rolling hills watching the glittering blue water with the white waves washing on shore. The sun twinkling on the ocean and I was sure I heard birds singing all around me.

It was on one of our escapes as we were walking hand in hand, that Kenny put his arm around me and I received my first kiss. It was right out of the movies. My head was spinning, my heart beating and I was floating on a cloud.

However, nothing stays the same and I have absolutely no recall of the end of my first crush but I always knew that this was someone I could never bring home or talk about with my family. I am sure that it was all over when he went to Washington High, two blocks up from Presidio and I went off to the only academic high school in San Francisco, Lowell High School. The high school of my father, sister and Steve after me. Tradition they call it.

Sadly, I learned many years later that Kenny went off to war and lost one of his arms. I was saddened by hearing that story. He remains in my heart and memory as my first kiss. As an aside, I believe he actually married Annie!!!!!

BROADWAY, HERE I COME…

Or, so I thought! Dazzled by my new professional dance studio, I found a place to be creative, hang with the "real" dancers and spend hours during the week floating on air,

Mr. Kahn and his wife, Pat Mason, were the owners of the most professional dance studio in San Francisco. Mr. Kahn, tall, handsome, kind and always congenial, made us feel like we were, and always would be, dance sensations. Miss Pat was petite and pretty but what a dictator teacher she was! As the ballet teacher, I was glad I did not have aspirations to be a ballerina. I even flunked toe shoe auditions.

Entering our studio made me feel so grown up. It was on Market Street, downtown San Francisco. The studio was upstairs from the Embassy Theater. Each time I walked under the marquee, I would picture my name in lights along with Gene Kelly or Fred Astaire.

To be in the dance room with wall-to-wall mirrors, ballet barre and a real living piano player (no, not a pianist) to accompany us made me feel like I was Cassie, from "Chorus Line." I loved my fantasy world and it took the pain away to pretend.

In a little side area between the box office of the Embassy and the door we entered to go to the studio was a tiny counter only cafe. The proprietor ran the shop by himself and always waved to me as I walked in the studio door. He always looked tired and worn but had a nice smile for me. Little did I ever imagine that he was the man named David that became the famous owner of David's Delicatessen, across the street from the Geary and Curran Theaters. His restaurant was the place to dine on Theater Row for celebrities and well-known San Franciscans. No matter when I saw him, he always had time to say hello and flash his little smile. Normally, he had that rough exterior of an immigrant in America. However, he proved once again, that in America hard work can make miracles happen.

Back to the studio. It was really scary to walk into the side door of the Embassy theater, walk down the creepy corridor and debate if I should take the dark, scary elevator or the two flights of dirty and smelly stairs. Hard to believe these days that young people could take a bus downtown, take classes and grab a bus home when it was dark without parents panicking. That was the way it was years ago, safe anywhere.

I danced with Mason-Kahn studios through high school. With the exception of the few years when Mr. Kahn suffered a heart issue and he brought in another well-known teacher, Glen Shipley. Glen had the bragging rights being the dance teacher and film choreographer for Vera Ellen. It appears that at one time there was a love interest between the two. We seemed to sense it from the look on his face every time he said her name.

Meanwhile, my dance style got better and better. I moved up from class to class. My repertoire now contained tap, ballet, jazz and chorus line. To say I was totally distracted by my dance and performance world would be putting it mildly. School was a far second in my everyday world. I had an ambition to go to Broadway and be a musical show choreographer. I still believe I would have been if only......

My high school, Lowell, as I mentioned before, was an academic high school. We followed a legacy and our entire family went to Lowell. It was on Hayes Street in the old Haight/Ashbury district of San Francisco. We were the Lowell Indians, our cheer was "give them the ax and our colors were red and white. Our music department was a block away in what we called "The Shacks." I played violin in the school orchestra. I would bribe friends to carry my violin case since I didn't think carrying a violin case was very cool. My violin playing days were very short. Although, I did join the violin section of the orchestra at my graduation for a performance.

We had an amazing drama department led by Mr. Polland. His claim to fame was having Carol Channing in his drama classes. Carol Channing was a proud alumnus of Lowell. In one of her last performances in Sacramento at the Music Circus Pavilion, I took the Red and White centennial yearbook to show her the page about her and have her sign my book. That was an experience after many decades. Our variety shows and plays were widely attended and many successful musicians and performers came out of our drama and music departments.

In my sophomore year, I started a chorus line known as "The Lowellettes." I stole ideas from my studio, taught my girlfriends routines and created some pretty terrific costumes. We performed at rallies, shows, city shows and hospitals.

My very best friend, Patti, and I were the same height and we were holding up each end of the chorus line. One year we performed in a major city-wide variety show. We were very excited that the "Lowellettes" were invited to perform. Being full of fun and excitement, Patti and I went to a florist, ordered American Beauty roses in a pageant bouquet, signed cards from a fictitious talent scout and sent them to ourselves at the performance. We gave specific directions to the ushers to present them to us at the end of the performance while still on stage. I don't need to tell you that our shock and surprise, as we accepted our rose bouquets, was worthy of an Oscar. We are still friends today and when we get together we always talk about it and collapse in hysterics at our guts to do such a thing.

I mentioned earlier in this memoir that my sister and I performed the famous Ted Lewis routine "Me and My Shadow." We had the pleasure of meeting Ted Lewis at San Francisco's Bal Tabarin nightclub on two occasions. During those times, he was kind enough to give us some tips on how to flip our hat during the hat tricks and we seldom dropped our hats when we performed.

Eventually, Glen Shipley opened his own studio in Daly City. It seemed a good time to make a change and I joined the new studio.

Although Beverly and I danced as a team for years, it was not her first interest. We were at an age where my dad gave us an allowance of $5.00 a week. I told my mother that I wanted to take a private lesson with Mr. Kahn. The next week, she went to our lessons with us.

When we arrived at the studio, mother said "Carol, go ahead and arrange your private lessons and give the office lady your $5.00."

I was so excited as I said to the receptionist, "Isn't it nice that I have an allowance and my mother says I can pay for my private lessons."

"How nice that you can do that", said the receptionist. "Mr. Kahn will be pleased to work with you."

She lined up my lesson times and gave me the schedule. I was so thrilled that I ran to my mother, handed her my schedule which she tucked in her handbag.

Then, she stood up, walked to the window and said, “I want Beverly to have private lessons too and I will be paying for them.”

Once again, I felt like a balloon lying on the floor, completely deflated. It happened again, Beverly had paid voice lessons. Now she would have private dance lessons. Years later, when I asked mother how she could do things like that.

Her answer was “Carol, someday you will know the importance and meaning of the attachment between a mother and her first born.”

It didn’t make sense then and it doesn’t now. It was just her damaged behavior from being the part of a three-girl family.

That is the beginning of my dance life. The next chapter will be the end of the story

Hugging Ted Lewis with appreciation for the “Me and My Shadow Coaching.

Costume #1 and Costume #2

58

THE GREAT WHITE WAY BECKONS

Coming back from the dance convention was always a difficult reality. Studies, responsibility, chores and more. I could feel the stardust whooshing past, dimming the luster from my eyes.

I was a dancer and that was my life and my goal.

However, there was a surprising phone call in our home one evening. I listened as my mother answered the phone.

"Who is this?" she questioned sounding as though she was annoyed by a nuisance call. Then she softened and answered "Oh, yes, I remember you. You are asking me what? That is very interesting but I will have to discuss it with her father before I say anymore. Thank you for calling and I will get back to you."

After hanging up the phone, my mother called me to join her in the living room.

"That was Evelyn LeMone from The LeMone Ballet Company in Pasadena," she explained, "She asked if we would consider allowing you to join her ballet company?"

I was stunned and as excited as if I were asked to dance with Mikhail Baryshnikov. After the first shock of the call, I was certain that my parents would not even consider the offer.

At the time, I was attending college in San Francisco, majoring in Theater Arts. I knew that I was not a ballerina and felt that I was as interested in ballet as Joe Montana (spectacular 49er Quarterback) was in playing baseball. However, ballet being my short suit in dance, I knew that time at a ballet studio would round out my dance resume. I always remembered my heartbreak, as an eight-year-old, when I auditioned to get my first toe shoes and I didn't qualify.

After several days, I was stunned to learn that my parents agreed to let me go. It was not until many years later I learned that my parents did not agree at all. I would have liked to be a fly on the wall during that discussion. Allowing me to leave school, go to Southern California, live on my own and make my own decisions was unimaginable. They had problems when we went to sleep away Jewish camp.

Visiting Pasadena and looking at what was available and safe for their daughter, my folks decided the YWCA was the safest place for me. They knew that I would be at the studio most of the day and how much trouble could I get into after I returned to my room exhausted? That was a very good speculation as my adventure began. Not a reality but a good try.

The ballet studio was exactly as you might expect. Springy dance floors, dressing rooms askew with dance bags, random types of leotards in every state, various types of ballet slippers and toe shoes strewn about, used towels, hair wraps and scraps of lamb's wool toe coverings.

The rehearsal room was filled with dancers in leotards and tights. The sound of the metronome on the piano keeping the beat, the twirling of toe shoes, the jetes and plies, the called directions of the ballet mistress. I was in heaven!

Then, I met Evelyn's son, Larry, a dancer but a jazz dancer. You can imagine it did not take me long to be in the studio with him working on choreography for a modern jazz routine or two.

What a relief it was for me, a true hoofer, to be able to break away from the rigid demands of classical ballet. Since all my days were spent in the studio, you can guess that my favorite time of the day was spent with Larry.

Word spread quickly that there was a new addition to the company that didn't seem to be the ballerina type. This new person appeared to be a tap dancer of some skill and quickly found her way to the modern jazz section of the studio. Yes, that was me doing anything possible to avoid another rigid, strict, demanding ballet class. Surprisingly, something rather exciting came out of my skill set. I was approached by Ted Howard, the choreographer for the newly formed Walt Disney Mickey Mouse Club. He was looking for someone to be his assistant and get the kids ready for their new show. Remember, this was the unknown group of kids starting the Mickey Mouse Club. No one had ever heard of Annette Funicello, Bobby Burgess, Darlene Gillespie, Sherry Alberoni or any of the other participants. I just thought I was training a young group of tap dancers. Imagine my surprise when a few years later, the M-I-C (see you real soon) K-E-Y (Why? Because we like you!) M-O-U-S-E Club took the country by storm.

I am sure every youngster in the country was saying, "Here's my ears."

Several years ago, at a dinner in my home, I was telling the story of the Mouseketeers and training them. My youngest son, now a grown man, stated that it was the first time he ever heard that story. Having a very keen sense of humor, he gave me a Mickey Mouse T-shirt for my birthday and a fresh set of "ears."

Every evening during my time in Pasadena, I ventured back to my room at the YWCA. Slowly, I began to make some friends as the residents from both the YWCA & YMCA gathered at one large table in the cafeteria. Once introduced, I began joining them in the evening when I returned home. That is where I learned about real life and it certainly wasn't the fairy tale that I had been living. I certainly learned much more than dance routines.

As luck will have it, I became acquainted with a young man from a very lovely family in New York. His father had a very successful business but before he would allow his son to join the corporation, he wanted him to spend a year or so on his own, across the country, to see what he could do on his own. We were like two lost ships at sea and we found each other. We had so much in common and didn't seem to fit with this eclectic group at the Y. We were inseparable and longed to be back in our usual environment. His friendship was just what I needed and I began to miss some rehearsals. Little did I know that behind my back the plot was thickening.

DANCE 10... FUTURE 0

With theater going on all around me, my desire was to pursue a career as a choreographer on Broadway. Everything in my life took second place to dance classes, rehearsals, costume fitting and performing at every opportunity.

The costumes, the scenery, the make-up, the props (sounds like song lyrics!) were so exciting for a young dancer. Mr. Kahn taught me a specialty number to "Satan takes a Holiday." I was costumed in florescent orange trimmed in purple sequins with purple plume feathers on the back. I loved the number until I appeared at a beautiful Catholic church for their Christmas show. I launched into my tap dance and as I moved into center stage, there before me sat the Priest, with a look on his face that made me feel that I was dancing right into Satan's den. My head starting spinning and so did I to get off that stage as fast as possible.

Years continued in the same routine, parents nagging about my studies and me dreaming, as though I had stepped into Vera Ellen's shoes and there I was dancing with Gene Kelly. I entered college as a theater major and continued to pursue my career.

Each year there was a dance convention in Los Angeles and all advanced and dreamy eyed dancers headed to the event. I was attending with my dance troup, of course, my mother would attend as my chaperone. My dance troup was Eldon and Irma Erwin (brother /sister combo), my partner, Valgene Allen, Benny Smith (he later was the choreographer for the Miss America pageant) and his partner, Shirley.

One evening while we were doing our routines from the day session outside of the pool area, we finished a number and heard applause from the second-floor balcony.

"Where is that coming from?" Benny said with excitement in his voice. Looking around, we saw two men smiling at us. They walked down the stairs to chat with us.

“Hi kids, I am Johnny Carson and I host a daytime game show. I really enjoyed watching you,” he said as he seemed to want to know more about us. “What are you doing down here?”

We told him “We are at a special dance convention for teachers learning new techniques.”

He said, “How would you kids like to attend my television show tomorrow. Here is the information

and we will watch for your arrival.”

We were so excited but did not have a clue who he was and what the show was about. However, we decided we were going to miss our session the next day to watch a television show being made. Little did we know, that we had met the future Mr. Television...the one and only Johnny Carson, the future night time host of “The Tonight Show.”

I returned home more determined than ever to head for the great white way and be the buzz of Broadway as an award-winning choreographer.

Posing in our garden before a performance

"Devil Takes A Holiday"
I really tried to vamp it!

Putting on the Ritz

AND SO IT BEGAN…

As I began to write this chapter, I glanced at the calendar tacked next to my very messy desk. It was July 25th.

That day would have been my father's one hundred and eleventh birthday. Interesting that he is the main character in this chapter.

As I mentioned several times before, the pharmacy was the center of my father's existence. It was a movie set of an old-fashioned corner drug store of the era. Green and White tiles covered the outer walls below the display windows, across the windows and a neon sign above the doorway advertising "Lloyd's Pharmacy." No, my dad's first name was not Lloyd, but Martin. He purchased this store from a Dr. Lloyd.

Walking through the wrought iron and glass doors was like entering a fantasy land for us as small children. To the right, racks of comic books, on the next wall, a huge candy case with every type of candy you can imagine. Across the way, covering the length of the store, a fully supplied soda fountain. Large containers of multiple ice cream flavors and the capacity to order milkshakes, sodas and sundaes.

Across the back of the store was a large divider wall with glass windows at eye level and the word PHARMACY across the glass. My father would walk out from that area in his white pharmacy coat, a warm smile on his face for all. He was always happy to see his children in the store, after all, we were usually sleeping when he arrived at home.

My dad had a collection of what we called "Damon Runyon" characters that hung out in the store. You could always find one or two parked on a tufted seat at the soda fountain. They claimed to be watching out for my father. As you can see by this long introduction, my young memories of days at Lloyd's Pharmacy were magical. It was a place where I could find my dad and have time to chat.

Now, back to the story of when my life path changed forever.

I had no idea that my dance coach and Ballet Mistress contacted my parents informing them of my lack of appearance at rehearsals. I found out very quickly when I answered the phone one evening and it was my dad. He instructed me to pack up my belongings. He had enough of what he considered nonsense and was bringing me home. He advised me that he was flying down on the weekend and I should be ready to leave.

This was a man that never left his pharmacy. He worked from 10 am to 11 pm six days a week. He would only work from 10 am to 6 pm on Sunday. He was an absentee dad. If I needed to speak with him, I had to call him in the store.

He was a loving man and provided a beautiful lifestyle for us. However, to this day, I am still not sure what the role of husband and father actually is supposed to be.

Suddenly, he was taking action and I was shocked and heartbroken. Where was he when I needed to be told by my father that I could be anything I wanted to be? Too busy with his customers to make it to a school play, dance or piano recital or any proud occasion. I was stunned to hear that he would leave his store for several days to fly down to Los Angeles to escort me home. I think it was the first time that he was on an airplane.

The evening before I left Pasadena, Lee and I spent a last sad evening together. I told him that I would be back and to show my integrity, I gave him my favorite stuffed animal to hold onto for me. I assured him it would not be the end for us or my dance career.

The next morning, my father waited in the cafe downstairs while I collected my things. I returned to San Francisco teary eyed and devastated, feeling as though my life was over.

You cannot begin to image, unless you have experienced it, how difficult it is to step back into the world of your childhood after you have lived in the real world.

As I previously mentioned, my father's pharmacy was across the street from the Jewish Community Center. Since my life was no longer my own, my dad talked to friends at the Jewish Center and I found myself not being able to refuse to work for them at their lobby desk. I worked a split shift 12-3 and 6-11 so that he could take me home when I closed the building. I was under surveillance at all times.

The Center was an architecturally magnificent building. It was at the corner of Presidio and California Streets and at the end of the California Street cable car line.The building was a hub of activity at all times. The entry lobby was lovely with tile floors, palm trees appropriately placed and a welcoming setting. I was the person behind the large, marble topped reception desk. I was taught to use a switchboard (if you can remember such a thing). Lily Tomlin and I truly had something in common. "one ringy dingy"…..(You had to be there to appreciate it.)

I reacquainted with my school friends, got back into a familiar social situation and the Southern California situation grew fainter each day.

Upon receiving a lovely wedding invitation from my girlfriend, I was so excited to ask Lee to come up and attend the event with me. We were thrilled to have a chance to spend some time together. Needless to say, my parents were not thrilled with the idea and asked me not to plan to host him in our home. They accepted the situation and tried to be cordial while disapproving all at the same time.

Our time together ended up being a disaster. I had become the obedient child, with no mind of my own, back in the pattern that prevailed all my life. I reacted to Lee very badly. Lee did not bring a suit for the Wedding, he had slacks and a jacket. Already inappropriate in my world. Suddenly, no matter his background, he wasn't a fit on my home turf. My behavior was unacceptable to me but I wasn't the same women he cared about any longer either.

I was torn in pieces and found my imaginary place of peace in a velvet light green pea-pod where I could pretend to be hidden. I had lost my courage, strength and would do whatever anyone wanted, not make waves and become invisible. That lasted over fifty years.

My mother, never a support system, resented that I was in the house again. It was a nightmare to be back in her home and I had to find a way to move on. I knew that the only viable escape for me was to find a nice Jewish boy and get married. I didn't have what it takes to disrespect my parents. Maybe generational or maybe cowardly, but it was the only available role for "a nice Jewish girl from a nice Jewish family."

As the world turned, so did I. Stoic, strong and serving others, my mantra for survival. Carol was no longer an individual. I was doing what was expected of me and I believed it was easier that way. Also, not true. The cage rattled and I thought the key was lost forever.

MIDDLE

"You don't start out writing good stuff.
You start out writing crap and thinking it's good stuff,
and then gradually you get better at it.
That's why I say one of the most valuable traits
is persistance."

Octavia E. Butler

WHEN CAROL GETS MARRIED

It is 1978 and I am moping around the house, on the job and knowing that I had only one choice to move on with my life. Each day, I would awaken, dress for work, shlep to the Jewish Center, take the bus home for my break, bus back for 6 pm shift and walk over to the drug store at 10 pm to ride home with my dad. Boring!

Meanwhile, days passed at the Lobby Desk. One evening, a few men came in to play basketball. One of the men plopped his gym bag on the counter and asked a question. He was very cute but so arrogant and not very pleasant. However, even with his rude behavior, there was a bit of a spark. He returned each week after that first encounter much friendlier and eventually asked me out on a date. Of course, I accepted.

You see, he was not a stranger. Our families lived on the same street, attended the same synagogue, with seats behind each other and our fathers did business together. Was that made to order? Okay, it didn't have much to do with love but it had a check mark on all the criteria. In the old country, it would have been the perfect match made by Yenta, the matchmaker. In fact, arranged might have worked out better.

Eugene was the youngest of three sons. The first in his family to attend college. His parents were immigrants from Lithuania. His father started a wholesale tobacco and candy company by visiting a retail store, taking an order, running to the wholesale house for the goods and delivering the order the next day.

Melvin, Eugene's dad, loved to tell the story of renting a small storefront on Fillmore Street in San Francisco. He took the cash he had and went to purchase his first inventory. He proudly took it to his shop and securely locked it up for delivery the next day. When he arrived the next morning, he was stunned to see that the shop was broken into and all his inventory was gone. His only option was to take orders, go buy the merchandise and deliver. Drive and determination made it possible for The Melvin Sosnick Company to become the largest tobacco jobber in Northern California and Nevada.

With Eugene's status as youngest of three sons, he was the crown prince of the family. Although he was only 5' 8" he was a small college All American Basketball player. His team nickname was "The Big Inch" because he could get around the taller players so easily. Eugene was over-indulged and horribly spoiled growing up. He was very fortunate, by the time he was high school/college age, his parents could give him all the benefits of wealth that were not available to his older brothers. It was in Eugene's world, an expectation and never considered a privilege.

Melvin enjoyed his alcohol a bit too much. Each evening, he would have his employees stop by his office for what he called "a little snort" before going home. It certainly did not please the wives of the men but they could not say no to their boss.

Unfortunately, it was a habit that Eugene decided to emulate when he had his own branch of the business in Sacramento and his alcohol consumption became a real problem for our marriage. With each and every hangover, Eugene's alibi was always a migraine headache and not the drinking. I was still quite young and came from a family with a magnificent neon lighted bar in their rumpus room but not a single family member was a drinker. The bar was only open for business when we had guests or hosted a party.

Eugene had been married before. His college girlfriend found herself pregnant, a difficult situation in those days. The only acceptable option was to marry as soon as possible and make a home for their child. David was Eugene's first born and the marriage lasted for a short time and ended in divorce.

When I started dating Gene, he was only a visiting father. David and his mother, Nita lived in Stockton. Gene would ask me to drive with him to Stockton to visit David. What I wasn't prepared for was his request to drop me on a street corner, go pick up David and come back for me. He didn't want to upset his ex by having someone with him, like David wouldn't tell her. Wouldn't you think that would have been a giant red flag for me?

To add to our connection, Gene went to College of the Pacific (now University of the Pacific in Stockton) with my first cousin, Wally. We had many acquaintances in common, albeit, older than me. While our families had totally different lifestyles, I knew that this was the path of least resistance for me. A nice Jewish girl pleased the Sosnick family, as well as the connection with my family. I kept telling myself that I could make anything work. Like creating a delicious cake, find the right ingredients and, voila, a perfect cake. That goes to show how young and stupid I was not having a concept of what happiness might be for me.

Some years later, a therapist asked me why I married him.

I replied, "He was Jewish, handsome, from an acceptable family. I knew I would never be a burden to my family and I guess I loved him."

"In that order?" my therapist inquired.

Our families coming together was the Jewish marriage of the season. Our wedding was held at the Fairmont Hotel, atop Nob Hill in San Francisco. The Venetian Room for the ceremony was filled with a large heart shaped chuppah (canopy) of white orchids, the aisle standards filled with an orchid covered heart of purple baby orchids. Followed by a reception in the Nob Hill Room with dinner and dancing in the Gold Room. Breathtakingly beautiful.

When I entered the Venetian Room with my hairdresser to take a look, I panicked.

"Please Merritt, take me away from here. Let's go now quickly," I begged.

Imagine I might have been the first runaway bride!

"Sorry Honey," Merritt answered with his arm around me, "You should have thought of that sooner. It is too late now."

Our honeymoon at the Royal Hawaiian Hotel can only be explained by the fact that on the fourth day, I packed my suitcase and asked for my ticket home. It was the first and last time in my life that I have soaked a pillow with tears. Considering that I would have to face my parents, of course I backed down and went forward.

We were in San Francisco just five months when the family purchased a tobacco business in Sacramento and gave it to their favorite son, sending along a trained salesman to assist Gene. Ironically, the one relative I had living in Sacramento was my dear cousin Wally and his wife, Arlene.

Wally's family was in the movie theater business and he had the movie houses in the Sacramento area. Arlene and Wally welcomed us into our new town and we met many young marrieds that remain friends today.

Soon Gene's ex and her son moved to Sacramento adding another dimension to our already spilling over plate. Mrs. Sosnick (not me, his mother) only discussed with me the fact that I needed to replace what was missing in Eugene's life, his son. Of course, being the third (actually fourth) daughter-in-law, it was required that I do what is expected. I have to admit that being a mom was not the first entry on my top ten list but thank goodness it was my path and I was blessed with fine children.

On February 10, 1961, I had an emergency cesarean delivery and Craig Stuart arrived on the scene. Since he was more than a week late, he was a nice sized baby of 9 pounds, 12 ounces and a handsome child.

Having a cesarean birth was quite a shock. I was in the hospital being induced when I received a phone call from my doctor telling me that I was having surgery in the morning. I was unable to have a normal delivery.

Panicked, I asked the nurse, "I am terrified. I didn't even read the chapter in the mother-to-be book. What is going to happen to me?

To add to my anxiety, here is her reply, "Oh, my dear, don't worry. Many times both the mother and child survive."

I called my doctor to ask if there was any possibility that I could go into labor that night. His response was not a chance in a million. I went to sleep feeling assured that it would all go well. In the middle of the night, I was awakened with such pain and thought my nervous stomach was acting up. With the next pain, that lifted me off the bed, I rang for a nurse and a team came running. In a flurry of activity getting me ready for emergency surgery, I asked the nurse to please not call my husband.

With such a look on her face, she inquired, "Why are you asking me not to do that?"

I simply told her, "Because I am not able to get off of this gurney to let him lie down so he can handle the birth of his child."

More than seven years passed, Gene was out almost every night with his boyfriends (should I have been more aware?) and I was busy being a philanthropist and a social butterfly. A live-in nanny took care of the children. I kissed them good morning when the nanny brought them to me clean and fed and I kissed them goodnight after their bath and ready for bed. Not a role model mother was I? How all that changed.

What a terrible mental battle I struggled with each day. Gene had always threatened me that if I ever left, I would not be allowed back in the door. That kept me in the situation much longer than it should have existed. When I realized that the environment would not be good for my male children, I gathered every ounce of strength that I had and left my home. I moved back to my parent's home and prayed that Gene would come to his senses and want us to come home. Let me remind you that his family was two doors away!

I guess in my naivete, I imagined our parents would intervene. Talk sense to Gene and try to get us to stay together for all our sakes. Instead, Mrs. Sosnick insisted that Eugene stay at their home and eat with them when he came to visit the children. As expected, Gene came by after dining with his parents to say goodnight to Craig and Joel. The next morning, he stopped in to say goodbye when he left. All it did was drive a bigger wedge between us. You see, I was not allowed to be in their home.

To quote my father-in-law, "I can understand that you would leave if there was no money. With all the money, you should be staying."

It did nothing but make the separation more difficult. Prior to my leaving to return to the Bay Area with the children, Gene took away the house, my car and replaced it with a salesman's used car. I was given $400.00 a month to raise my boys and they had $150.00 each in child support. That lasted until they were teenagers with nary another dollar given.

One day, it was necessary for me to ask Gene for some information. I called the office and asked for him.

"Is this Nikki?" the woman answering the phone asked.

"No, it isn't," I responded."

And the rest is history. Not a good history or worthy of space in my memoir. I was a single mother, with two sons, 21/2 and 5. Now let us see how strong I could be during this new way of life.

FAMILY members were first to learn of the engagement of Carol Gay Aizenberg and Eugene S. Sosnick at a dinner given by her parents, the Martin Aizenbergs.
Bill Cogan photo

Engagement
Announcement

TOAST TO BRIDE—The former Carol Gay Aizenberg became bride of Eugene S. Sosnick in ceremonies at the Fairmont Hotel recently, with a reception after in the Fairmont's Nob Hill and Gold rooms. The bride, daughter of the Martin Aizenbergs, attended S. F. City College.
—Du Charme Photograph

February 21, 1959

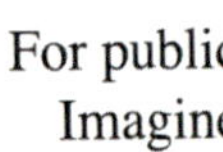

Wedding Photo

For public
Imagine

Entertaining at home "An Evening in Bavaria" before we crashed!

SURPRISE, I'M A MOM

You get married and the first question that greets you after "Hello, how are you?" is, "When are you starting your family?" That was a challenge for me since it was not my first priority.

I can't say what the priority was but it wasn't childbearing. That changed abruptly when Mrs. Sosnick, a very controlling mother-in-law, told me over and over that I had to replace what was missing in Eugene's life. He had a son from his first marriage and it was my obligation to provide him with another son.

What a joke that was for me. I don't think it was ever important for Eugene to be an active father except that it would validate his virility. What did I know as a young woman leaving the safety of my family home to marry the boy next door and Jewish "catch" of the community?

But out of everything bad comes something good and I was blessed to have that come true for me. On February 10,1961, Craig Stuart arrived by emergency cesarean section and I became a mother.

In those days, we did not learn the gender of our child until the day of their birth. Lucky for me, I delivered a boy and the family rejoiced. In spite of the emergency surgery and a 6-day confinement, the Brit Milah (ritual circumcision) was scheduled on the traditional tenth day.

As the family stirred around our home preparing, I was struggling to accommodate the demands for platters, trays and serving pieces needed for the feast after the ceremony (like I could think about food when my child was about to traditionally become a Jewish male and cry because something hurt). Never a comfortable experience for babies but a must for Jewish males. My memory of that day was my mother and mother-in-law fighting over which one made the best honey cake. I was glad when that day was over.

Craig was adorable and I suspect it was because he was ten days late and beautifully formed with enormous blue eyes. Mrs. Lawson, his baby nurse, was a true gift for me. She taught me not to be afraid of motherhood but it was certainly a switch from a life of luncheons, parties, manicures, facials and whatever had my attention for that day. Now it was Craig and the mystery of raising a human being. Funny, I would probably be tying his shoes to this day if a "How To" baby book did not instruct this new mom what comes next.

The years would be eventful, filled with much more good times than problems. Craig was a very good child. Always independent and that has never changed. He gave up his bottle at 7 months old. One day, I can't remember his age, he pulled himself up on the laundry basket and walked with it across the room. That was exciting!

It all went so fast—the first day of school, an amazing Bar Mitzvah, Boy Scout Pinewood Derby (I was so bad at it, competing with the dads, we finished last.) And then came the dreaded day, the acquiring of a driver's license. I still worry!

We even established a yearly tradition. When Craig was about 7 years old, his favorite birthday dinner was homemade spaghetti with a Canlis salad. Canlis was a restaurant in Hawaii that Eugene and I visited on our honeymoon. Their salad was fantastic and I brought home the recipe that became a standby of mine for entertaining. Craig's request each year on his birthday was Canlis salad and spaghetti. I believe we did that each year until his thirtieth with only missing one year. For his birthday several years ago, I gave him a salad bowl, salad servers, the ingredients and recipe for the salad. Like most of the "special" recipes, when you try it yourself, it isn't the same. Of course, Craig called me a short while after his birthday to report that he tried and failed to make the salad and it just wasn't the same. I don't believe he has ever tried again..

Craig was very artistic. He loved drawing, creating projects and, most of all, costumes. His costumes were always a hit. The epitome was when he wanted to be Gene Simmons of the rock band "Kiss" and we managed to do it to perfection, make-up and all. I had always hoped that he would pursue his talent as an artist but he was too much of a "jock" to put anything before sports. Be it basketball, baseball or football, Craig was a sportsman first and foremost. Lucky for him, his father had access to the best tickets to all local sport events and he always included Craig.

Among my most treasured memories with Craig was our sneak aways to the Oakland Coliseum. After he came home from school, he would do some homework then we would give each other that look, throw on our Oakland Raider fan gear and head out to the game. We didn't care about homework, school the next day or anything else. We would drive over the bridge, grab a hot dog and cheer our great team to victory. Those were the days!

With the success of the Sosnick tobacco empire and the family encouraging Craig to skip a readily available university education and immediately join the company, it was a difficult offer to refuse. I hoped that Craig would take a few years and expose himself to other opportunities. My brother jumped in and advised me to let his father guide him and stay out of it. I gave in to the expected behavior of the times and kept my feelings to myself. That is a regret that I have always had tucked away. Who knows what might have been if he left his options open?

Craig's strong suit was always his "cut to the chase" realism that made him the person to see if you had a dilemma. He, in three sentences or less, could point out the solution that you were struggling to find. To this day, he is my point person for clearing out the smoke screen and making sense out of a problem.

Although Craig and I have had some communication issues, we recognize it is simply the complication of two independent, complex and strong-willed individuals that just happen to be mother and son.

I am so proud of the man he is today. Self-directed, confident and he asks for nothing but to be respected and loved. He has built a wonderful life with Christy, her children and grandchildren. Their life is thoughtful and caring. I remember years ago that I read somewhere that the greatest gift you can give your children is wings to fly and follow their dreams. While I have hidden in the shadows and finally found my authenticity, I am grateful that I have been able to give him the independence to be the authentic, fine man that he is.

Yes it was really special to be a mom

Isn't he Adorable? I'll have to fight off the girls when he grows up

Craigs Bar Mitzvah What an emotional and beautiful day!

Well here is Mr. Sports

How did so much time pass so quickly - Craig is 30!

YES, I DID IT AGAIN

I find it hilarious that when you have your first child and go through the birthing process, you know that you will never do that again. However, time has a way of taking away your consciousness as you enjoy the raising of your first child and cannot wait for the next one.

Knowing that I didn't want to raise an only child, the time was right to complete our family.

Becoming pregnant was not a problem for me. I used to joke that if a sperm was tossed in the air, it would find me and I would be "with child." Happily, I was expecting a newborn in July. This time, fully prepared for the scheduled cesarean delivery. We lived in Sacramento long enough that we were friends with our doctors and knew we were in good hands.

Getting close to my due date, during a doctor visit, Dr. Marv informed me that he had to make a trip to visit his ailing mother and he wanted to do the surgery before he left. I believe I was due mid-July but he scheduled it for July 5th. I worried a bit that it was early but it had been a healthy pregnancy.

Being a holiday weekend, my parents and in-laws arrived to see me off to the hospital on July 4th and be present to welcome their new grandchild the next day.

I was all prepared with my long, dark hair done in a French twist, a fresh manicure and pedicure in firecracker red for the occasion and dressed in a blue denim sleeveless maternity dress with a red, white and blue scarf dangling from the pocket. Very bravely, I hugged my family and off Eugene and I went to the hospital.

I walked into the hospital excited and felt quite elegant as I readied for my newborn and the luxury of surgical delivery with no labor pains. That was before I found out about the second baby afterbirth discomfort. Just one surprise after another.

As I followed the directions and got into bed to settle for the evening,

"Nurse Ratched" appeared with her hands full of prep tools. I smiled a friendly hello but this lady was not friendly.

"I am here to prep you for your surgery," she bellowed like some drill sergeant, "Get those pins out of your hair. Here is nail polish remover for your fingernails and toenails.

Call me when you are done and I will return for the rest of the preparations."

With tears in my eyes and enraged by taking away my egocentric image of how the elegant lady should be ready for her "confinement," I began to remove the pins from my hair and counted each one matching my tears. As for nails and toes, what a mess removing red nail polish can be. I think I was now so nervous, I had red marks all over everything. Not an auspicious beginning to Joel's arrival but I pulled myself together and as I was rolling to surgery, I managed to smile and wave at the good doctors.

My second son, Joel Howard, arrived July 5, 1963 at 7:57 a.m. I had returned to my room after delivery and was a bit groggy and uncomfortable when the door to my room opened and in walked my mother, father, mother-in-law and father-in-law all talking at once.

Trying to always say the right thing, I uttered, "Now I have my doctor and my lawyer, aren't I a lucky mom?"

If you didn't have the impression already that I didn't have an authentic bone in my body, now you could see it for sure. No tears, complaints or acting as though I had just delivered a baby and wanted to sleep, always mind your manners and please others.

Joel arrived at 5 pounds, 8 ounces but lost weight and was 4 pounds, 14 ounces when he was allowed to go home. I was so happy to have him and went down to the nursery window so many times each day. The nurses in attendance were so used to seeing me viewing the baby that they left the shade by Joel's bed raised so I didn't need to bother them during my multiple visits. He was so small and always smiling. Here is the entry I made in his baby book at nine months:

Joel is the most unusual child. So bright and cheerful, quick to smile and very responsive. He wants to be part of the family unit, and plays well with Craig without fear. He has an unusual way of making his desires known. He is a pleasure to have, how lucky we are!!

On 08/28/1966: *I am sitting and glancing through this book tonight and cannot help but pause and make another entry after reading the above. Joel is now three years old. He is everything above and more. He continues to be the joy of existence and can bring pleasure to the darkest of days. He is cute, clever and has an insight beyond his years. He possesses that quality that sets certain people apart from others. His growth shall continue to bring added amazement (with G_d's will). I am truly blessed.*

There is another entry from 07/21/1970. It is long and revealing. It speaks to Joel's growth and interests. Craig and I were very devoted to him. Joel loved animals and especially our pet dogs, Snoopy and Trinket. I learned that Joel was aware and able to make good decisions and did very well without his "helicopter" mom who needed to take a step back.

My final entry from that time is as follows: *What can I say except that G_d gave me the very best two sons that He had to give life.*

Joel has always been so sensitive to situations and other people. In elementary school, he had a girlfriend and he gave her his I.D. bracelet (a fad of the day) and she became his one and only. That lasted until his boy-friends teased him. He came home from school one day, closed himself in his bedroom and cried.

When I knocked on his door and asked what was wrong, he said, "I took my ID bracelet back today and hurt someone's feelings." With tears streaming down his face he said, "My buddies teased me so much and I wanted it to end so I broke up with her and she returned the bracelet."

While I have hovered over Joel since his birth, it has taken me many years to realize that he is an adult male and doesn't need his "mommy" to fix everything for him. Like any mother, I want to step in front of Joel and protect him from anything that may cause him to be unhappy. Isn't that silly for someone who never aspired to wedded bliss and many children? Funny, like the nurse in the hospital told me when I had Craig, trying to assure me: I would never hurt my own child. She knew how frightened I was of caring for a living person that I carried for nine months. But once you hold your very own child in your arms, just know that it is the most difficult moment to let them go—and it is a moment that seems to always arrive too soon.

Real life is not Hollywood and what is supposed to happen usually doesn't happen. However, true happiness is satisfaction with what you have. Many years ago, I read a passage that stated the best gift you can give your children, if you are blessed to have them, is wings to fly and their independence.

Motherhood is a gift. Courage is the biggest asset when raising your children. As you stand by and watch them blossom into fully functioning adults, there is a sense of great pride and a small spot in your heart where you keep your baby in your arms safely tucked away forever.

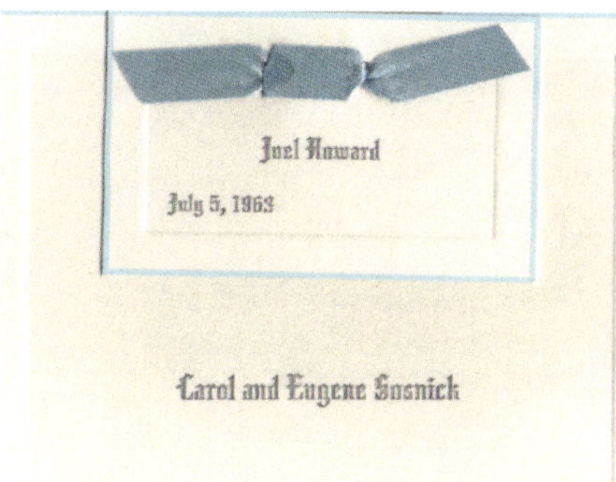

Birth Announcement - I think Joel was born with a smile

Adorable and a very kind boy

A very nervous young man but a wonderful job was done

Graduation - What will the future hold?

A celebration and we have this special picture of us

THE COURAGEOUS, COWARDLY LION

Now that is a contradiction, isn't it? Let me explain, psychics tell me that with my birth date and time, I am a Leo, with a Leo rising sign and my moon in Leo. Of course, that doesn't mean much to most folks, however, I like to use any crutch I can to make sense of my life of peaks and valleys. Being centered is a challenge for me since the frivolous elf on my left shoulder is always in conflict with the wise owl perched on my right shoulder. All in all, it has taken a lot of years to ride my merry-go-round of ups and downs as my story unfolds

Yes, there I was living in my beautiful Sacramento home knowing that I was preparing to return to San Francisco. I went to a moving supply store and purchased all the same size boxes and packed them each day. When packed, I would stack them inside a closet so that Eugene would not have to be made uncomfortable watching us prepare to go. Thus, all the same size boxes.

I had Eugene's shirts, suits and sport coats freshened, shoes polished, and organized every dresser drawer so that he would be able to function on his own. Each category in the closet was hung by color. Wasn't I a silly woman, why would that make me feel any better? All Gene needed was his Tanqueray gin, sport events and men friends to enjoy life and it was all good.

On moving day, I took my two sons, our clothing, daily needs and headed to my parents' home in San Francisco. Their three-floor spacious lovely home allowed us to be there but not under foot. Once again, their daughter returned home. This time with two children.

I spent several months with my parents. I mentioned before that my parents and in-laws lived one house apart. Even being there for some time did not improve, in any way, the situation with Eugene's infrequent visits or my relationship with the Sosnick family. I was persona non gratis. It took me a long time to realize that Gene was much happier without the responsibility of a family.

After looking for a place to rent, I found a gorgeous condo in Diamond Heights. It was a new subdivision built on a hillside in the city with a panoramic view of downtown. As the sun set, the view came alive as if we floated in a sea of twinkling lights and we would sit and watch the show.

I made friends with another young mom and we would walk our children together and chat. My children's ages were $2^1/_2$ and 5 at that time. I enjoyed that location until the day that Joel fell off of his tricycle and nearly rolled over the ledge to the patio of the condo below us. That did not bode well for this being a permanent location.

Several days after the episode with Joel, my neighbor friend called me.

She had a question for me. "Is your ex-husband Eugene Sosnick?

"Yes," I replied, "Why are you asking?"

"You won't believe it," she responded, "My mother works in a very high-end boutique downtown. Yesterday, some woman rushed in, dragging her daughter behind her.

She announced loudly so the entire store could hear, "My daughter is marrying a very rich man. We have a credit card in his name, Eugene Sosnick, and she is to buy anything she wants."

Remember the time I called Eugene in his office and a lady asked if I was Nikki. That was the woman that could have anything she wanted while I was raising the children on $400.

When they left the shop, my friend's mom called her and told her the story. For some reason she was able to associate the name with whatever my friend had told her about me.

To say that I was shocked would be an understatement. I still had a slight flicker of hope that Gene might come to his senses and want to have his family back.

Although my condo was gorgeous, I was driving the children across town to school each day. I wanted to be closer to family if I needed any help at all. I relocated to a flat in the Anzavista neighborhood, halfway between two of my dad's pharmacies.

After six months, it was time to go to court in Sacramento and get the final divorce done. It was a miserable day, perfectly fitting for the situation. Not being very savvy about being head of household, I went along with Gene and agreed to use the same lawyer for the negotiation. Another ignored red flag! I met the attorney, Seymour at the courthouse and we went to our designated courtroom. As luck will have it, I knew the presiding Judge and was very embarrassed.

Looking down at some paperwork, Judge Perluss questioned, "What is the reason for this divorce?" I could see his discomfort.

I answered, "Eugene does not want to be married anymore."

With that, the Judge gave his gavel a strong bang and declared the marriage over.

But I was not done with the day yet. Expect the unexpected.

Seymour suggested that it would be a good idea to grab lunch before heading back to the Bay Area. I was feeling so shaky and agreed it might give me time to settle down. Lunch was pleasant enough until the entree plates were removed and we were waiting for coffee. Suddenly, Seymour threw something in front of me. It was a key and I didn't have a clue what it was so I asked.

He smugly said, "All divorced women are lonely and need a man. It is a motel room key."

I almost returned my lunch I was so insulted. We were friends as couples, attended the same synagogue and raised our children together. A divorced woman, no longer just Carol, a friend. No respect, no dignity. I was devastated.

"How can you treat me like that when your wife and I are dear friends," I admonished him.

"Oh," he smugly replied, "Always worth a try."

On my ride home, I had plenty of time to think about the need to protect my children and give them a good home but I felt so unsure of my ability to make everything right. I was venturing on my first real experience of being all alone, with many people buzzing all around me. People, people everywhere but not one to help.

The realization that I had to go to work to support my family was a puzzlement. I had no idea what it was to maintain a home and be the breadwinner. How far could $400 go? As I was raised, I had no idea what things really cost. Eye opening and scary.

I decided to go to a quick program to get a job as a medical assistant. Uniform, no work clothes to purchase and I could work part-time and be able to get my kids to school and pick them up. Welcome to the real world. What I did know for sure, was that I wasn't going to let my parents take care of me. Craig and Joel were MY children. I took them in my care alone and I was going to make it happen. A Coward, yes, terrified. Courageous, you bet.

SINGLE PARENTING IS UNDERRATED

Realizing that being a single parent was a challenge and, most certainly, in the years I raised children alone. It was not a badge of honor. Still, I knew that my children would have a chance to be in a healthier environment than staying in the existing situation.

Did I make the right decision? I doubt myself sometimes but I can say that I have two sons that make me very proud. They stood on their own feet and came to be fine men, while the projection for children from a broken home was dismal.

We made several moves before we landed in the right place. We ventured back to the Bay Area and settled in Burlingame, a half hour from grandparents in San Francisco and near my sister and her children in San Mateo less than ten minutes away. I was so proud to be able to purchase a home on my own merit without a cosigner (quite an achievement for a single woman in the seventies). The charming home had previously been a tea house on Burlingame Avenue, on the main shopping street, and was moved to the current location.

Our home was within walking distance of good quality schools and down the hill from our synagogue, Temple Sholom. The boys went to Hebrew School to prepare for their Bar Mitzvot at age thirteen and attended Sunday School. They excelled at sports and joined Cub Scouts. Even while working, I was able to be a Den Mother and proudly walked in parades with my sons and our scout troop. We had so many good times. We created the best ever haunted house on Halloween and even turned our home into a movie theater including curtains and a candy counter.

Our adventures were many. One day, Craig, Joel and I were walking across the schoolyard by our home. We were probably heading for an ice cream cone and waving at friends. The next day, Craig came home from school not very happy about something. Seems one of his friends had something to say that bothered him.

"Hey, Craig," his buddy commented, "I saw you, your brother and sister walking across the schoolyard. Where were you going?"

Craig answered in a sarcastic tone, "I do not have a sister. That was my mom."

"Oh," replied his buddy, "Sorry about that. I thought it was your sister."

Craig was quite dismayed and didn't find it at all amusing. Still, having a five-foot mom, in jeans, tee shirt with her hair in two pigtails could easily be mistaken. I thought it was hysterical.

My boys were sports fanatics and I became a jock too! I attended more sporting events than ballets and washed more mud-stained clothes than I ever imagined I would.

The kids were avid Oakland A's fans during the glory years of power and handle-bar mustaches. Often, we would be sitting around after school before deciding to head to Oakland at the last minute to catch an A's game, even on school nights. I must admit it was fun to hang out with my sons and we grew up together.

We made decisions together, no second parent voice. Cried and laughed, got hurt and stayed well, had tonsils removed, shared simchas (Hebrew: happy occasions), achievements large and small while enjoying our version of family life.

We were one happy little family, with all the usual ups and downs. We hung in together and created a bond that I never thought could be broken.

Off to the debate

All my favorites in the park together

Lena & Sam got married and we had fun!

My handsome men

Cruising together to celebrate birthdays

Stephen Aizenbergs 60th Surprise b'day

WHEN CAROL GETS MARRIED, PART II

Let's bounce back to San Francisco for a little bit.
I will remind you of when I worked as a Medical Assistant at a doctor's office on California Street, between two of our pharmacies. To move forward, I must take you back to that time.

One day when I was working in the front office of a medical practice, a lovely young woman and her mother came in for an appointment. The appointment was for the daughter. I noticed what a strong resemblance I had to her. Small stature, dark-haired and Semitic looking. There was no question that when her mother opened her mouth, it was a Jewish family. It appeared that we could do nothing right for the mother, from the wait time, to the type of reading material and how stuffy the office felt. I could see there was no pleasing her and couldn't wait for them to go to the treatment room before we had to handle a patient mutiny.

At the end of that long day, Dr. Bachman called me into his office. I stepped into his office with hesitation wondering what was on his mind.

"I am here," I said quietly, "Is there something special you need me to do for you?"

"Just sit down in the chair and be comfortable," he said, while rubbing his hand over his forehead, seeming distressed.

I had no idea what was bothering him so much and sat waiting for him to speak.

With a slightly choked voice, he finally spoke, "How do I tell the mother of three young daughters that she is dying of Cancer?"

I was stunned and inquired of him, "I am sad to hear this. Will she have enough time to raise her children?

With what appeared to be his last show of strength, he almost whispered, "I don't think that will be possible."

I saw the entire Recabaren family once more when they came in together for a final conference on care and treatment. A sad group trying to handle such a heartbreak.

I never had a follow-up since I left the medical practice a short time after that to move to the San Francisco Peninsula. A much better climate for my boys that were born in Sacramento and the climate was not good for them in the city. We were always in the Pediatrician's office for endless ear infections. And that is how we ended up in our unique home in Burlingame.

Our life in Burlingame was fast-paced and fun. The boys were always busy with their sports. Much more than their books, I might add. Our home was originally the Burlingame Tea House on Burlingame Avenue and it was moved to the current lot some years before we became the owners. It was charming with a pot-bellied stove in the kitchen to keep warm, a winding staircase leading up to the bedroom area, a separate area over the detached garage for a play-room and lots of asphalt for a basketball backboard to keep the boys busy. What a great house!

Before long, it was nearing B'nai Mitzvah time and we were commuting to the synagogue three times a week for Hebrew and Sunday school. I decided it was a good idea to move closer to the temple and make our lives easier. Within a few years, the boys would be going to Mills High and time to relocate. We found a wonderful home in Millbrae, it even had a swimming pool. Not a usual home accessory for the area.

During that time, Craig was an active and creative teenager. His actions gave me many laughs and, at times, the urge to send him to the moon. Always being ambitious, he had a paper route. Each day, the stack of papers would be at the curb waiting for him. He would fold the papers, rubber band them, fill his carrier and be on his way. Being a very independent child, he wanted to handle his responsibilities on his own. He did not appreciate suggestions and rejected support. I left him to it until the day of the big surprise.

I was always fighting with the boys to clean their rooms. That never went over well. One day, while the boys were in school, I decided to take on Craig's room for a thorough cleaning. He had quite a nice room with the window facing the street. A built-in desk, bookcase and a large closet for all his extras. His closet had sliding doors so you could only work on one side at a time. I got to the closet part and opened one side to check his clothing and make sure it was in order. That done, I moved down to the other side. I slid open the door and was buried beneath an onslaught of undelivered newspaper inserts that were so heavy I fell to the floor. I was furious! Imagine all the sales that were missed by subscribers and how about the cost to the advertisers. That paid for the newspapers and Craig's paycheck. Craig simply didn't want to bother stuffing the papers prior to delivery. What did I do about it? Nothing, it wasn't my job or an argument that I could win.

Wait, there's more. When Craig turned sixteen, it was Learner's Permit time. Like all other teenagers, he could not wait to drive. I made sure to give him private lessons since it was not something I could handle and I was sure a professional driving teacher would do the job in a way that worked for Craig. He seemed to be a sensible driver and I trusted him. Until the day I received a call at work that Craig ran into a parked car on his way home from school. He was busy waving at his friends to make sure that he was being seen and forgot that he was steering a car. What did I do? Nothing, another no-win situation. I was so grateful that he could drive and help with errands, a bit of a dent was acceptable.

Sometime later, I had my typical day. Work, go home, fix a meal, check on homework, clean up and when finished, sit down and read the evening paper. While glancing through the social section, I noticed a beautiful picture of a bride and groom. The caption read "Linda Recabaren, daughter of Ernest and the late Marilyn Recabaren and Robert Wilbur etc. etc. I had been so curious about what happened to that family. Now I knew one of the three girls had married.

Still, curiosity got the best of me and one evening I decided to call the Recabaren home in San Mateo. After several rings, a man answered.

I said bravely, "This is probably the strangest phone call you have ever received."

He responded, "Try me. I get some pretty crazy calls."

I explained to him that I had worked for Dr. Bachman when his wife was ill. I remembered Marilyn and her mother and recalled the day they received the diagnosis.

Then I said, "I really just wanted to know how a family carries on after such a difficult loss. I saw the picture of Linda as a bride in the newspaper and I could not resist calling.

To this day, I cannot recall if Ernie asked me out at that time or if we spoke again, and then he asked. But within the next few weeks, we had a dinner date planned. I dressed very carefully for the date. The A-line dress was the fashion of the day. Mine was red plaid, with a large white collar and a black satin bow at the neck, black patent-leather ballerina flats with my long dark hair pulled back with another large black satin bow. The doorbell rang, I opened the door and this is what I heard:

"Oh no, I have two more just like you at home."

That was the start of eight year of dating. Ernie was father to Linda, his married daughter, Susan, a typical middle child, and Christine, who became my darling daughter of another mother to this day. She was so young when I came into her life and she was a gift to me. We did girl stuff, worked together, dressed in the same color on holidays. You know all the things I couldn't do with two boys. When Christine was engaged, I was able to help her plan her special day and be a mother of the Bride. We had a wonderful time.

Still, I would not marry Ernie, nor would we live together. I wanted to raise my sons without conflict or confusion, or so I hoped. Ernie rented an apartment not too far from our home. He would spend time with us but always go home. The only full-time we had was when Craig and Joel were in Sacramento visiting with their dad.

One day, I had a phone call from Linda, Ernie's eldest daughter. We exchanged the usual pleasantries and then she explained that she wanted to discuss her father.

With underlying anger, she stated, "My father loves you so much and he wants you to marry him. You keep turning him down. Why is your religion and lifestyle so much more important than a happy life with my dad?"

I attempted to explain, "Linda, I am a divorced mother of two sons. My first obligation is to raise them to be good men. I don't have time to indulge myself at this time. Maybe someday I can consider what works for me too."

Our phone call ended shortly after that and I kept hearing her comment in my head. It took a different turn of events to make me change my mind.

During the holiday season that year, I had to run by Ernie's apartment to pick up something.

I checked with him at work to see if it was okay to go by his place. No problem for him but it turned out to be quite a problem for me.

On his couch was a collection of Christmas presents. Ernie always mentioned that he wanted a black tie with white polka dots and I just never remembered when it was gift time. There upon his stack of gifts was a box with a white shirt and black polka-dot tie. Atop the gift was a card and it read "Ernie dearest, here is what you always wanted. Love, what ever her name was." Suddenly, I was green with envy, red with rage and lost my cool. Against my good judgment, I agreed to marry him a few short weeks later.

Ernie was so pleased that he was agreeable about everything. He went to see my Rabbi to discuss the path of conversion to Judaism. It didn't seem to matter to my parents, they still would not sit in the same room with him.

After I said yes, Ernie stopped by my store and gifted me with a lovely engagement ring. We arranged a wedding service in the temple courtyard and a reception around the pool at my home after the ceremony. It was a very nice day.

It was only a few weeks before I realized that I acted in haste, knew better and made a big mistake. Sometime later, I decided to attend therapy sessions to understand my new circumstances. My therapist explained that it was a marriage that could never work. He educated me to understand that Ernie, as the middle child of three sons, simply was attracted to a familiar situation in his relationship with me. He assumed the middle child role in my household, resenting my two sons. Craig represented his older brother and leader and Joel was the little brother that got the attention he wanted. Now, I was the mother of three sons. We tried it for several years and then had to give up.

However, there was a big gift from the situation: Christine, the youngest daughter. She was my daughter of another mother and has lived in my heart to this day. We have remained in touch and experienced much during the years. While I would have loved having her live close-by, she has always lived in Michigan. We have maintained a long-distance connection.

Here are two quotes from Ernie that I have never forgotten;

"I love you more than life itself," he said quite firmly, "I just can't stand to be in the same room with you."

"In my next life", he snidely commented, "I want to come back as Carol's poodle."

Wouldn't you think that I had enough. I tried and failed again. Enough was enough or so I thought.

Love to be a bride!...

...What was I thinking?

WE INTERRUPT THIS MEMOIR

It seemed a good idea to take a break and bring you, dear readers, a little insight into where this memoir is going.

It is January, 2020. A new year and a new decade. I am the almost new and improved person that I have strived to be. The cage is still unlocked.

Last year was six months of transition from taking care of all humanity to finding out that there is something called self-care. What???? I never heard of it or had a clue what it meant. I do recall my mother always calling me selfish. That seemed like something terrible to be. I never wanted to be whatever selfish meant. She just neglected to tell me that it was okay to recognize that I existed and had needs and wants like everyone else.

We all experience lots of emotions during holidays and 2019 was not a banner season for me. It came so quickly the world situation was chaotic and created anxiety. It was a holiday I could not wait to get over and begin 2020. I thought that sounded like a number for a good year. Was I wrong!

I decided to gift in a way that was different than overloading my sons with stuff they didn't want or need. I baked my "World's Greatest" chocolate chip cookies and gave them to those that made a difference in my life in 2019. That included my favorite checker in the grocery store, the kind lady that bagged the groceries and took the basket to the car, the money collector freezing in the cold booth at the entry/exit to my doctor's office building and the helpful manager at our neighborhood "Tuesday Morning." Okay, you get my drift. It was a holiday to remember those often-forgotten individuals that make sure we are taken good care of on our visits.

I still felt the loneliness of the season. No grandchildren to surprise with their special wish, sons and their significant others too busy to worry about mom, It was awareness of what is real in life and what was a fantasy when I was growing up. It was a missing link not to have children at home any longer. No brisket and latkes (Hebrew: pancakes) with family gathered around the dining room table eating and laughing. Just another day, another time. I could not wait for 2020 to arrive and I had my bucket list ready.

Let's resume the memoir so you can fill in the blanks and know the reason for this break and why I needed to write it before we moved on together. Let the stories begin.

ESPECIALLY FOR YOU

Having been raised in a family business, my entrepreneurial spirit had me imagining a new type of business every week.

As I went from one retail management job to another, I felt that I needed to express my own creative talent in a more challenging situation.

Remembering the amazing personalized gift shop I visited in Southern California, visions of names and initials on lucite engravable items floated in my head like sugarplum packages at Christmas time. In the 80's, personalized gifts were few and far between.

Doing my daily chores of parenting, working, cleaning, shopping, cooking and the endless "mom" tasks, I was busy planning my next move. I found an office, a very small room with a restroom/storage space and nothing more than a spacious display window for street viewing. The rent was affordable, my inflated desire to make it happen and with enough good credit to get a decent loan for set up and merchandise.

Jumping through the start-up business steps, I couldn't wait to get the paperwork approved, my business license, shop cards and buying at the San Francisco Gift Show.

The day finally arrived to head to the city by the Bay. When I entered the Moscone Center in San Francisco, I felt like Alice must have felt when she fell through the rabbit hole. I could not believe the sight in front of me. I truly felt as though I was in Wonderland. Before my eyes was every gift, gadget, game and more. I didn't think I could see it all in one week. Lucky for me, I had a theme and while I could gaze at every item you could imagine ever owning, I knew my direction.

This dreamer could manage to find every engraving type of tool to personalize anything. I selected a hot-stamp machine, an engraving machine that looked like R2D2, every gift I thought I could engrave, gift wrap, ribbon and on and on. Thrilled with my shopping trip, I dragged myself home with a briefcase full of orders, machinery information and my dream was ready to be assembled.

The store came to life with shelving, signage, a stunning black and white striped awning over the outside display window, red geranium wallpaper covering one wall and two small display cases. Oh, I forgot to mention that the shop had no back-room or space for equipment so all machines were delivered to my home. The dining room became my workshop.

Each evening when I closed the store, I would transport orders and stock; do the engraving after serving the boys dinner and pack the finished merchandise into my car. After the boys left for school, I would jump into my car and race to the store, haul in the merchandise and gift wrap it. At 10 a.m, I would unlock the shop with a big smile on my face and begin another day of names and initials. I was finally self-employed. My best seller was imprinted cocktail napkins and I must have stamped hundreds each week. At $6.00 a hundred, it was a best seller.

Within the first year, business thrived. Personalized gifts were really special. People in the community that never spoke to me started to drop into the store. It didn't take me long to realize that they wanted a freebie for their next fundraiser or a job for their daughter. My sudden popularity was underwhelming, to say the least!

My greatest challenge was teaching myself to engrave on R2D2. I can't begin to tell you how many mistakes I could not sell that I use in my home. I just tell people it belonged to a relative and they gave it to me. However, my female brain helped me engrave in ways that the manufacturer never thought of putting in a manual.

One day, a customer came into the shop and ordered a personalized lucite clipboard for a popular San Francisco television celebrity that appeared nightly on a talk show. How nice I smiled at my customer, not having a clue how I was going to engrave a name at the bottom of the clipboard. Believe it or not, I did it upside down and backwards to have it right. Shortly thereafter I heard that she presented it on her show.

"Look at this," she said waving the clipboard in front of the camera, "Isn't it great. I understand it came from an adorable boutique in Burlingame called "Especially for You."

I almost fainted with excitement when I heard about it. Soon the phone was ringing off the hook and I engraved clipboards, upside down and backwards, for weeks on end. It was a crowning moment for me and my brain child of a business.

Within a year or so, a mall was built where the old Burlingame Avenue movie theater used to be. It was called "Fox Mall." It was time to expand and I moved the store to Burlingame Avenue, the main street, and inside of Fox Mall. I joined with about ten other creative merchants inside the mall and we really complimented each other. It was a very good time.

For our grand opening of the mall, my son, Joel, costumed as a fox roamed the town all day. It turned out to be a very warm day and he was so hot and sweaty. It was a great day for me but I don't think Joel has forgiven me yet for the gig.

Business was wonderful for many years and suddenly interest rates on loans jumped to 22%. My banker stopped by the store one day and just threw out that he thought I should consider using my savings to pay off my store loan. I worried and really did not have anyone to discuss it with so I panicked, ran to the bank, took out what was needed from my savings and paid the loan in full. It made things a lot more difficult to have to start worrying about business and not be doing just the fun stuff.

I was also becoming a bit tired of doing the same thing over and over. I had my fun and now it seemed that some of the joy had diminished. How could it not when this became my day-to-day in the store.

The phone would ring the moment I opened the door and I would answer, "Good morning Especially for You.

"Hey, Carol, this is (fill in the blank). I am going to a luncheon today at noon and need a hundred cocktail napkins in yellow and green as a gift. Imprint them with Tom and Carolyn. I will pick them up at noon and make sure they are nicely gift wrapped with your special paper. Thanks, bye."

That was the usual call, not even 24-hour notice. Another clever game was going to Menlo Park to the Grainware Outlet, a lucite factory and shop the sales.Then, bring them to me to engrave. It was infuriating since I carried the regular line of Grainware in the store. If I damaged their item during engraving, I could not take one off the shelf to produce without an error. Didn't take me long to set a policy of not engraving outside merchandise.

Five years passed and all I heard from the ladies was, "I am just dying to own an adorable shop like yours."

I wanted to tell the envious ladies what it took to have a "cute little shop" like mine. I had gotten to the point where a mere piece of tissue paper torn or wrinkled and unable to be used could move me to tears. Dusting the merchandise each day, unpacking and marking orders, taking out the garbage, paying bills, shipping and the beat went on. It was all wearing a bit thin. The end product was great but getting there was doing me in.

I had a lovely lady come in to cover for me once in a while but mainly, on Tuesday morning. That was my manicure day. I was certain that if I didn't walk in the back door of I. Magnin at 8:30 am on Tuesday, the building would collapse.

When I returned to the store, I would inquire of Jan, "Did we sell anything good."

"Of course not," she would answer, "They look, but only buy when Carol is here to make sure it is exactly the right thing."

Better I should have opened late on Tuesday. It wasn't too long before I decided to close Especially for You and move on to see if there was going to be anything Especially for me.

Especially for You
GIFTS

10-27-79
With Love
Mom,
Congradulations
on the excellent
store.

THE ROAD RUNNER

After years of running my own business, I found that I wanted to be free from the daily grind of running a shop. I decided to go to work selling merchandise to other merchants that could maintain the dusting, cleaning, public demands, overhead and all the parts I didn't know about when my dream shop "Especially for You" was just a dream, and not a reality.

By this time, Craig decided to forego college and go right to work in the family business. It was the Melvin Sosnick Company, wholesale tobacco and candy, with locations in Northern California. Many years had passed since the divorce from my son's father and Sacramento was still the location for the branch of the business that was run by Craig's dad. Before I was ready, out flew the first chicken from my nest. Not an easy transition for me since raising my boys had been a dedication. I took them out of their extremely privileged life that the Sosnick family offered them when we were together and that which was denied after I was gone with the children. Guilt was now a companion to my fear.

I began to hunt for a job checking in with all my favorite vendors on the gift market. I hit it lucky and landed a territory with a gift vendor in San Francisco. Our showroom was in the San Francisco Gift Mart and my responsibility was San Francisco. You cannot begin to imagine what challenges life on the road in San Francisco can present.

Each day was like Christmas in my home with my front porch filled with carton boxes. My samples had samples. I found myself stocking, labeling, packing, filing, creating binders, breaking down boxes, packing my car and there I was, having a boutique in my home that needed to be inventoried, priced up to date, orders sold and tended to daily. Whatever made me think it would be easier! Not to mention, the ability to be self-disciplined and get out on the road each day.

I dragged sample bags, long before bags with wheels had been created, up and down some of the oddest staircases in the back of shops in the city.

Note that shop owners were not of the gentlemanly persuasion and never offered to help. Since my samples were books, greeting cards and assorted games, I developed superwoman muscles but couldn't get bigger than a five-foot pack mule size.

Gift shows involved setting up our booth days before the opening, seven day show and endless booth break down the last day. There were times at breakdown when we waited hours for the union workers to bring our packing containers. They came by the luck of the draw. The show shut down at 3 pm and we could wait until nine in the evening, and even later, to get them. I vividly remember being so tired and trying to pretend that I had the stamina of the Eveready bunny. That worked until I picked up a porcelain musical figurine, it slipped out of my hand and shattered like the implosion of a ten-story building. I sat myself down and simply sobbed from exhaustion.

At that point, my family had migrated to Sacramento. My Mother and Uncle Sam moved to be near my brother, Steve, a real estate developer. My nephew, Mitchell, my sister's eldest, attended McGeorge School of law. Slowly, I watched my entire family take up residence in Sacramento. I decided I would be in a better place if I moved back to Sacramento. More family life for all of us. Interestingly enough, within a few years, my niece Karen, her husband and children relocated to Sacramento, as did her brother, Gregory. Amazing, since it all started with my marriage and business being in Sacramento in 1960. Now, the entire Aizenberg family left San Francisco.

As luck would have it, I landed a territory job with a major vendor, the Roger Wilson Company, in the Sacramento area. What a step up from books and cards. The merchandise was so fun to sell. We had everything, games, home decor, stationary items, well, you name it and, at one time or another, we would have it at Roger Wilson.

My first winter road trip was really something. I finished dressing and got ready to head up to Grass Valley. It was a sunny day in Sacramento and off I went. As I started to pass one little town after the other, the sun went away and I was driving through a beautiful road of trees that resembled something I had seen on a Currier and Ives Christmas card. OMG, it was snowing. I was enchanted at first and soon became aware that I was cold and didn't feel comfortable on the road. Although I did not have an appointment with the best gift shop in Grass Valley, I slid in there, with my cotton slacks, summer blazer and flat shoes, apologizing for stopping and explaining my dilemma. They were so nice, made me a hot cup of coffee, looked at my samples and wrote a nice big order. You can only imagine how quickly I drove home after that stop.

Along with my road job, I decided it would be good to have a real estate license and help my brother with his corporate projects. Real Estate is not a career for gentle," save the world" oriented people. I tried it more than once but found it was just a very tough place for me to try and enjoy my work. Make money, yes, make friends, not so much. I continued to take ongoing classes to maintain my license, even though I couldn't imagine working in Real Estate ever again. One class was very interesting. I learned in that seminar that our brain has the capacity as large as the state of Texas and we only use 30% of it. I was also reminded that my mind does not think independently; it thinks what I tell it. You can program your mental computer and youwill get the result you want.

I decided to test that class theory on my next commute to work at the SF Gift Show for eight days. Instead of getting a hotel room and staying in the city, I wanted to sleep in my own bed at night and dress out of my closet in the morning. I got my car ready, packed morning and evening commuter snacks and prepared to try and see if I could program myself to do eight days of commuting without burning out. It worked, I loved greeting the day, the transition from hours of being inside a hall selling, breathing the fresh air and singing along with the radio. Munching carrots and celery kept my mouth busy and I was home before I knew it. That was before cell phones. It worked all week and I never enjoyed a gift show more. So much for the Traveling Salesperson.

Life sailed along well and I liked living close to my family. I had lots of choices when it came to spending time with them and I was able to share valuable time with my sons. Life passed with the usual patterns. I was single, had two poodles and a nice little condo. Since I made many adult friends when I arrived here as a newlywed, the renewed friendships filled my days. I continued to be a road runner. I felt I was settled in and took one day at a time. Never say never, I had no idea what a turn my life would take.

WHEN HARRY MET CAROL

The Summer gift show went on. The mornings were beautiful with an awakening morning shade of blue sky, the sun peeking through the puffy cotton ball clouds and I was happy as anyone could be that was driving two hours to the city by the Bay, working 10 hours and hopping into the car to return to my warm nest in Sacramento.

Feeling so happy and ready to meet the visitors to our booth, I was filled with fun and looking forward to greeting my customers. I spotted a gentleman walking into our booth and he looked somewhat familiar. Without being obvious, I pretended to be checking some display in the area where he was standing because I needed to sneak a peek at his show badge. Once I realized that I knew this man, I turned around and approached him.

"Hi Harry, how nice to see you in our booth," I said with my best stage smile.

Looking stunned by my approach, Harry responded, "Hello, do I know you?"

"Of course, you do," I snapped back, "we shared an employee. Sherrie Pappas was my assistant manager at Piccadilly and worked for you on weekends. By the way, where is the adorable Shirley?"

Harry looked at me with shock and his face turned a pasty color white. My stomach rolled over and I was aware that I said something very wrong.

"Shirley passed away last year in December," Harry answered, with a shaky voice.

I was so embarrassed but how would I know that? Fumbling along, I apologized and asked what I could help him with in the booth.

What was the first thing that passed through my mind? I realized that this was the man my psychic told me about the year before. Short man, short name...Harry Loew. Owner of Mr. H. Luggage and Gifts. Remember,

Stephanie, my psychic, said I would be carrying a suitcase with my initials on it. Time to reveal that years before when I was taking a trip, I went to a very high-end luggage store (not Mr. H.) and purchased a magnificent plush velvet French luggage set in a powder puff mix of pink, gray and white. I decided that I wanted my initials put on the bags and asked Sherrie if she would mind taking my new luggage and asking Mr. H. if he would imprint my initials on the bags in gold. I didn't think of it at the time of purchase and the fancy luggage store didn't even bother to suggest it. Harry agreed to do it for me.

Sherrie and I had such a close friendship, we could finish each other's sentences. Our years together at the Piccadilly store were filled with great times and many adventures. Sherrie had a daughter, Lisa, and she was the same age as Craig, my eldest. The children attended the same school and had some classes together. It was at the children's graduation party that I officially met Shirley and Harry. It makes sense that he didn't have a clue who I was when he saw me at the gift show! Sherrie took my luggage to the shop for engraving. Good thing we wore badges at the show or I wouldn't have remembered him either!

Back to the gift show, with our conversation going on, an entire group of mutual friends passed the booth and stopped to speak to both of us. I was quite amused by how many people we knew in common and not one of them would have ever thought to introduce us.

After writing a very nice Drueke game order and anything else I could convince him to buy, he was ready to leave. He hesitated for a second before he spoke.

"Let me know next time you are in town, we can grab a bite of dinner," he threw out into the vapors.

I chuckled and off he went. I met Harry and it was a good day.

That evening's ride home was filled with merriment. I was sure I met the person mentioned in my last psychic reading, and it was also a financially great day. The munchies tasted better than the days before and the music seemed especially fitting as I sang along. Home for sweet dreams.

AND I THOUGHT ABOUT HIM

The gift show was over and life was returning to normal, almost. I kept thinking about Harry and wondered if this was the person Stephanie was talking about. However, I was just so tired of being the nice, courteous, good girl that did the right thing all the time, I knew that I had to find the answer to what Harry actually meant when he left my booth.

He nonchalantly said, "Let me know next time you are in town and we can grab dinner."

I decided to take things into my own hands and find out. I made a call to Mr. H. Luggage store in Daly City. Without any trepidation, I picked up the handle of my gold princess phone and dialed.

"Mr. H Luggage," a lady answered efficiently, "what can I help you with today?"

I asked politely, "Is Harry available?"

"Sorry, he has stepped out for a few moments," she stated.

I left my number for him to call back. Much to my surprise, there was a call back within five minutes.

"Hi Carol," Harry said as if he were speaking to a sales rep.

"Thanks, Harry, for calling back so quickly," I stated with confidence. "I have a question to ask you."

"What would that be?" he replied, "Something with my order?"

"Oh no," I quickly replied, "I want to know what you meant when you said we would get together if I was in town. Did you mean you wanted to take me to dinner or 'Hey, Sweetie, next time you are in town, give me a call'?"

With a touch of humor in his voice, Harry said, "Do you want me to come to Sacramento and take you to dinner?"

Of course, I did, but I wanted to take things slow now that I was discovering making time for me. I answered, "Thanks for your response and clarifying your intention but I am not ready to do that yet. I just wanted to know what you meant. I will give you a call when I am ready."

With that, I hung up, resumed doing whatever I was doing before the call. I thought quite a bit about Harry. How casually I knew him, the many years my girlfriend worked for him. The luggage that he stamped with my initials. I remembered the luggage that I purchased from his shop when my sons were taking their first trip with their father. I gave them the luggage for Chanukah and knew that I had a picture of that somewhere. My guys in their footed pjs; holding up their new luggage. Where, oh where, did I put that picture? I hunted and found it. It gave me such pause to think about the coincidences in life and the miracles all around us.

God works in strange ways. When I finally felt the time was right for me, I would give Harry a call. Until then, I would enjoy the anticipation and not ruin the reality of what actually happens when you put yourself out there. Maybe this time would be different.

Harry even remembered the luggage prices.

STAIRWAY TO THE STARS

How often we dream about a magical evening, the dream date and it doesn't happen. Hollywood movies and Danielle Steele novels romance us into thinking that the knight in shining armor is right around the corner waiting for us.

However, I had my fantasy fulfilled and I am going to share it. If you are ready for the next Harry chapter, here it is.

Several weeks after telling Harry that I was not ready to see him at the time of our conversation, an opportunity came my way. As a road rep, I was always on call for any type of wholesale show scheduled that featured our products. There was a Tobacco Show in San Francisco for the weekend of my birthday in late August. We carried the fine line of Drueke games, top of the line walking sticks and ivory games by Comoy plus numerous other gifts for the high-end connoisseurs of fine tobacco products. I realized this would be a lovely time to make plans with Harry.

Then I went about planning my weekend in San Francisco. There is a lovely boutique hotel on Geary Street, right across the street from the Curran and Geary Theaters. The lobby is beautiful with marble floors, fine art and urns of fresh flowers in just the right places. They had a luxurious cafe with windows that opened to the street, weather permitting, so it felt just like a sidewalk cafe in Paris. It was going to be a birthday treat for me and I was excited. The Tobacco Show was on Saturday and my niece, Karen, was having a baby shower on Sunday. An exciting packed schedule for a birthday weekend. Such fun!

I called the Regent Hotel to make my reservation for my favorite room if it was available. Of course, it was and I couldn't resist telling them that it was my birthday weekend. After confirming my reservation, I was ready to call Harry to see if he was available. Oh, I forgot to mention that when I looked at the theater section in San Francisco that weekend, there was a fantastic show taking place at the Marine's Memorial Theater on Post Street. It was called "*Stardust*" starring Gloria Loring, an entertainer of song and movies. I wanted to buy tickets but thought I best call Harry first to see if he was available.

The next afternoon, I made the call to Mr. H. Luggage and asked to speak to Harry. I believe the same very polite lady answered the phone and asked who was calling. I was put on hold and very shortly Harry picked up the phone.

"Hi Harry," I said, with my heart pounding in my chest. "I have a plan to get together if you are available on Saturday, the 24th of August."

"Oh my," he said with some hesitation in his voice, "I am leaving for Paris on the 2nd but I think I can swing that. What did you have in mind?"

Realizing that he was showing a sense of humor when he said he was going to Paris, gave me a bit of a window into his whimsical side. Too bad, as time passed, that keen sense of humor disappeared.

Feeling a bit of excitement and thinking about the prophecy of my psychic, Stephanie, I was delighted to see if this was the one. Short, short last name, 5'7" and the last name of Loew. I couldn't wait to find out.

Sharing my plan with Harry, I rambled, "I have to be in town for the Tobacco Show on Saturday, then to a baby shower the next day." Babbling on, "I found a wonderful show in town called "Stardust" and I wanted to buy tickets if you are available that evening.

"Oh, I am so sorry but I can't do that," he answered.

I was crestfallen and said, "But you said you were not going on your trip until September 2. Why did you change your mind? Did I say something to offend you?"

With a bit of a jovial tone, he answered, "No, you didn't do anything. I just won't go with you unless I buy the tickets. It is your special weekend and I want to do that."

With a mixture of anxiety and happiness, I said, "You scared me. However, if that is the condition, I appreciate it very much. Let's talk next week and firm up the plans."

With that, I knew that this birthday would perhaps be the truly happy day that I always hoped to have each year. As I previously mentioned, I am a triple Leo, Sun sign, rising sign and my moon is in Leo. Leo people like to think that they are royalty and their day must be special. That makes my birthday a brass band day. I believe that as the clock strikes midnight on August 22nd until the clock strikes midnight on August 23rd, everyone has to be nice to me because it is my day, and mine alone, the one day of the year that no one can ruin. As it happens, now that it is 2020 and I am a senior citizen, I still feel exactly the same way and I celebrated "Covid" style. No party! Cake, candles, cards and flowers work!

With great anticipation, I started to plan my foray into the big celebration in San Francisco. Little did I imagine what a wonderful weekend it would be for me.

I COULD HAVE DANCED ALL NIGHT

As the big weekend in San Francisco approached, I busied myself getting ready to head into the city by the Bay. I selected my most comfortable and attractive business suit and very comfortable shoes to wear into the city. I wanted to "wow" my potential customers but nixed the high heels to survive the day.

Next, what to wear for my big date?

I decided on a special theater suit, black, lapels trimmed with decorative beads, dress heels with bead trim and a small evening bag. Ta-da! Dressed for San Francisco's theater scene I was piqued with anticipation as I put myself together for the weekend that had endless possibilities.

Saturday morning arrived and I was a whirling dervish. The car was packed, the sitter arrived for the dogs, my separation anxiety kicked in as I double checked everything. I checked five times and then again. I was a wreck.What was I thinking about making this date along with work? It would be exhausting! And my second thoughts began.

I finally dragged myself away from home and made the drive to San Francisco. I am surprised I got there safely I was so fidgety. Driving into San Francisco is like a magnificent movie set. As you go across the bridge, the gently swaying blue ocean is filled with weekend sailors. The water, a sea of white, billowing sails, Alcatraz on the right and the underpass through Treasure Island stretched ahead of me. The panorama of buildings, illuminated by the sunshine, welcomed me to the charm of the Big City.

I approached the Regent Hotel, pulling up in front, and was graciously welcomed by the doorman. My luggage was taken to the desk where I was greeted in a way that made me feel like a princess. The celebration was beginning.

"Welcome, Mrs. Sosnick, how lovely that you have decided to spend your birthday with us," the desk clerk smiled as she prepared my key and paperwork. "We have your requested room all ready and hope you enjoy your stay."

What a transition from my crazy day-to-day in Sacramento leaving me rung out and exhausted! I felt like Cinderella just arriving in my pumpkin coach.

Running late and having to get to the hall for the Tobacco Show, I rushed up to my hotel room. As I entered the room, there on the desk was an enormous vase of flowers and a fruit basket as a birthday gift from the Hotel. What a fantastic start to my day! Quickly unpacking my bag, hanging up my theater suit and putting my cosmetics on the sink in the stunning marble bathroom, it was time to grab a cab and get to work.

The day progressed with many visitors to our booth. I have very little recollection of that work day since as the hours passed so did my sinking feeling of dread. I remember my mother (of blessed memory) telling me:

"Carol, just remember," she would sternly say, "anticipation is better than realization."

I couldn't get that out of my mind. It was so much fun, for the weeks before this actual date, to day dream about what might be, could be or might not turn out to be. Dating in your mid years carried as much baggage as Harry stocked in his luggage stores. I really didn't want to have to deal with the reality.

The show was over, I grabbed a cab back to the hotel and was in a terrible state. I took off my jacket and shoes and plopped in a chair. I was filled with regret and started praying that Harry would call and cancel. What happened to my plans to rush home, remove the stale make up, shower, apply a fresh face and finish off with a soft spray of my Tiffany cologne?

Nope, not me. I sat in my work clothes, daunted with the idea of the evening and stubborn as could be. Time passed and I didn't move. Then the blast of the telephone brought me back to reality with a jolt.

"Oh no," I said to myself, "maybe I won't answer the phone."

Of course, I answered the phone and heard, "Hi, I am here." It was Harry. With joy in his voice he asked, "Do you want me to come up?"

"No," I almost shouted, "I will be right down."

There I was with the beautiful theater suit, sparkling shoes and delicate little evening bag still sitting in the closet. I ran into the bathroom, did a quick face touch up and another spritz of the cologne. Ugh, perfume over perfume. My fault, I sabotaged myself trying to avoid any disappointment.

Heading to the elevator, I was almost sick with nerves. Landing in the lobby, the doors parted and standing right outside of the doors was Harry. He had a gift bag in each hand. I was stunned. He had purchased perfume from Oscar De La Renta that filled one gift bag and the other contained all the little sample extras that salespeople like to give you along with your purchase. I thought it was so thoughtful and never wanted to let him know that my current fragrance was my one and only. Still, the gift cologne bottle, sitting on my vanity table, was a constant reminder of a fantastic evening.

It was one of those magical nights in San Francisco when the summer weather made it possible to comfortably walk around the City with a warm, soft breeze off the ocean making the temperature just right. We headed across the street to the lounge of the Clift Hotel on the corner. That location was the perfect place to start off an evening. With the soft music of a piano off in the corner, we enjoyed cocktails and shared appetizers. It was a perfect opportunity to break the ice and get to know more about each other. Having been a customer in his store, enjoying an acquaintance with his late wife, Shirley, and sharing an employee, my dear friend, Sherry, made it easy to exchange conversation.

As showtime approached, we left the Clift and walked up two blocks to the Marine's Memorial Auditorium. As we should have expected, we bumped into mutual friends. I knew the show would be enjoyable, I had no idea how romantic it was—or was it just the cocktails setting in?

When Gloria Loring entered the stage, I had to take a deep breath. She was stunning and dressed in the most beautiful coat I had ever seen. Straight out of an Erte designed masterpiece, the black velvet maxi coat with fur trimmed lapels and a wide rhinestone belt. It was breathtaking. Then, she began to sing, "I'll take a Stairway to the Stars" and I thought I would swoon in my seat. It certainly set the mood for this special date and I deeply regretted not being freshly in my theater clothes to fit the scene.

The show ended but our evening did not. Harry's next plan was to go to the Starlite Roof at the St. Francis Hotel and finish off the evening in a very special way. Yes, I could have danced all night but, instead, we did dance until it was time to close down the bar. I believe there was one other couple in the room when it closed.

With the weather still sultry, we strolled back to the Regent. I hoped none of the other pedestrians noticed I was walking on cloud nine!

I mentioned to Harry that I would call him before I left the City on Sunday evening and maybe we could meet and grab a bite. He hesitated a few minutes, made some type of remark and I could tell that it was as confusing an evening for him as it was for me.

When I awakened in the morning, I could feel that I was getting into that "polite, good girl" mode. I promised myself that the next man in my life would have to make the effort. I was through with making things happen for others and not for me. With that, I checked out of the hotel, attended the baby shower and drove home. It was the perfect date and I knew Harry was the short man with the short name that was going to be a big presence in my life. However, I wasn't making it happen.

My daily life continued with reminders around me of the great birthday week-end. The hotel flowers, the Oscar de la Renta perfume and samples, it was just the birthday I wanted.

Then I waited, Monday, Tuesday, Wednesday and I knew that good manners dictated a thank you. I was going to do it by mail. I went to the art store, purchased a small 5x7 inch canvas, black India ink, a fountain pen and more. I went home and got busy on my project by Thursday. I was sitting at my desk and had just drawn Gloria Loring in THE coat! It was a side view, with the right hand raised holding a sparkling star. The greeting read: "A perfect evening is climbing the stairway to the stars." As I was placing rhinestones one by one on the belt of the coat, my phone rang.

"Hi, how are you?" inquired a voice that I recognized.

Yes, Harry called! I didn't have to make the first gesture. I liked my new plan. How funny that it was right when I was setting "diamonds" that radiated the stars in my eyes.

"How would you like me to come up to Sacramento this weekend and take you to dinner?" Harry queried and I could hear the question mark.

"I had a very busy week but that sounds lovely," I responded.

We made our plans for the weekend and I plotted the path I was going to take with this new person. My normal behavior would have been to have his Scotch chilled and waiting for him after the drive and an array of goodies to nosh on. Not this time.

I sat in wait and when Harry arrived, I greeted him, introduced my menagerie and then proceeded to apologize for not having a bottle of Scotch or any nibbles for him. I explained I had a busy week on the road and didn't have a minute to stop and shop.

With that Harry said, "Not a problem, I will run to the store and pick something up. Do you need anything else?"

"Aha!", I said to myself. "This time it will be equal and I will count too."

The memory remains to this day as the night my daydream was answered. I walked the stairway to the stars and it was going to be a magical adventure.

Joy is a
Stairway to the Stars
Sprinkled with
Stardust

WILD ABOUT HARRY

To bring significance into the next 23 years of my life,
I want to introduce you to Harry Loew.
You need to know him to understand how I came to write this memoir.

Harry was born in Vienna, Austria, December 30, 1927. His father, Max, was the privileged son of a woman who ran the largest millinery factory in Vienna. Harry's grandmother was always a business woman and, as a result, the Loew family had special status in Vienna. I never heard a word about his grandfather. Nor were they involved in creating a Jewish environment for Harry.

Harry's mother, Rivka, was from a middle-class family, traditional in their religious practice. They gave Harry what little connection he had with his Judaism. Rivka was a seamstress in the hat factory and that is where she met and attracted Max. Max was quite a bon vivant and traveled all over Europe presenting their yearly fashion merchandise. From the impression I was given, Max led quite an exciting life.

Rivka was one of three sisters and the only one to have a child. Being the only child in the family, Harry was raised as the golden child with comfort and security. I truly believe that the beginning of his life as a dearly loved child gave him the strength to endure what was ahead for him.

As the Hitler regime started to rattle the sounds of a changing life-style, rumors began to spread of the terrible activities in other parts of Eastern Europe. Grandmother Loew felt, as a well-known business leader, she was not in the vulnerable segment of the Jewish Community. She lost her life in a camp that we were not able to identify when we searched records.

The rest of the Fuchs family fled very early, with the first threat of pogroms. Rivka's two sisters and their husbands found sponsorship and passage to America immediately. They settled in New York.

Max's brother left for Israel, taking family treasures with him. Their sister was able to go to England where she resided for the rest of her days.

Nothing more than that was shared by Harry and getting more information was difficult.

Harry was a happy, loved and clever child. His mother was alone so much she was able to give Harry a safe and secure beginning of life. When Hitler invaded and Vienna had military posts everywhere, Harry would ride his bike all around the soldiers like it was a game. He would even stay out after curfew to see if anything would happen to him. Growing up as a "golden" child gave him the idea that nothing bad could happen to him. That first five years of love and security gave him enduring strength.

When Max realized it was time to flee, it was very difficult to find an escape. After many attempts, he was able to pay triple the cost of passage to get someone to get them out of Vienna. In the dead of night, they were given passage to end this clandestine adventure in Shanghai. On the train through Siberia, Harry turned thirteen without possibility of a Bar Mitzvah.

Shanghai was a haven for the family in the beginning but that tide soon turned. Many of the people who fled Europe early headed for Shanghai. They established businesses and were very successful. However, they were not welcoming, nor concerned, with the refugees that arrived in droves later.

Harry's mother was very ill prior to leaving Vienna and her condition worsened as they traveled and arrived in Shanghai. She passed away within the first year in Shanghai. A devastating loss for Harry but he dealt with his life as he had in Vienna. Everything was a game.

The first few years, around 1940, the family was living in the French Concession and Harry was attending school. However, it was not long before the Japanese overseers gathered what they called the "stateless" people and placed them in a ghetto. Harry's father was devastated by the fact that he was privileged in the family business but was ill-prepared to find a way to survive. Harry seemed to be the father to his broken-spirited father.

Early in our marriage, I asked Harry, "Why is it that you never complain?"

His shocking answer to me was, "When you have been as hungry and cold as I have been, you are grateful for everything you have."

For a diaspora Jewish person, his answer stunned me.

Harry explained, "We would sit in a cafe until it closed to be warm. We would follow the coolie man with the buckets of hot liquid, having no idea what it was, just that it was hot."

Harry shared that one of the early Jews to Shanghai, who was very successful, gave Max and Harry a back room to live in. The room had broken windows and was scorching in the summer and freezing in winter. They would get in their cots and pile all their clothes on top of themselves to hope to be warm and sleep.

But Harry and his determination prevailed. He played soccer which allowed him to get out of the ghetto and compete with other teams. I have copies of the Shanghai Jewish Community newsletter (in Chinese) that gives details of Harry's success as a soccer player. To that end, the Jewish Soccer Club, Hakoah, in San Francisco sponsored Harry and his father to leave Shanghai and settle in San Francisco. Upon arriving in America, Harry was given a job working in a pickle factory.

Little did he know that American soccer players were not what he was used to being up against. He joined the team on a trip to compete in New York. His Fuchs family that had settled in New York excitedly attended his games. He was so beaten up after that series that he quit the team and thus, his soccer career was over. He secured a job in San Francisco at Granat Brothers Jewelry store as an apprentice. His father became the Theater and Music critic for the San Francisco Jewish Bulletin. Only in America.

How I wish he had stayed in the Jewelry business! The luggage business that he went into with his partner, Henry, was where he ended up. Now, that is carrying a lot of baggage!

As for me, Glitter is my middle name. My eye never missed a thing that glittered. Always sparkling was my life goal. My favorite wall hanging states "Eat glitter for breakfast and sparkle all day." Imagine how much of a surprise it was to find myself entrenched in the luggage business. I already had my own baggage, I never guessed I would be adding to that already overwhelming stack. That's life!

UNDER THE CHUPPAH

On January 10, 1993, Harry and I had a small, traditional wedding. Harry was shy about the event and only wanted to include immediate family in the ceremony and invite others to the reception in the evening.

We gathered in Sacramento, staying at my mother's home, where the ceremony would take place. The celebration began with dinner on Saturday night at the house. At 9 o'clock the next morning, the Chuppah (the tent that we stand under during the ceremony) builders arrived at the house to set up the cover and decorate with flowers. My mother's garden was filled with color as cheerful as a Monet painting. Mom greeted everyone with a delicious buffet set up for the family as they arrived.

By eleven o'clock, the outside was ready, we were enjoying bagels, lox and more. I was too nervous to eat and Harry was a wreck. Rabbi Moses arrived to do the Ketubah (signed marriage contract) ceremony. That is the document that is signed before the ceremony by Bride and Groom, and two witnesses, who declare that we will abide by the covenant that is described in this document. A beautifully designed document prepared to frame and hang in our home to remind us of the day that the bond was sealed.

Oh, I did forget to mention another very important cultural requirement that is dictated before we could marry! I was to get a "Get" which is a Jewish Divorce. I needed to go before a ritual committee of men at a conservative synagogue that would cast me out from the family of my children's father. A requirement only for the woman.

On a damp, dark evening in San Francisco, I went to Congregation Beth Shalom in San Francisco for this tribunal. It was eerie as I parked my car and walked by myself with only the light from the street light to guide my way. I sat cold and shivering alone in the foyer of the synagogue. Finally, a man in a kippot (head covering) stepped out of the inner office and told me to enter. A gathering of six men, heads covered and in dark suits sat in a semicircle. They asked me to stand at the back of the room and put my hands together ready to receive a document. I was terrified as I looked around the room of the aged temple. Cases of Holy books, pictures of religious nature all about, dank and a bit eerie. I did as I was instructed and they asked me to slowly step forward toward them. When I reached the designated destination, the Rabbi proceeded to caste me from the Sosnick family. I was never to be aligned with them or be part of them. I was instructed that I could not marry again without the written permission of my ex-husband. You can just imagine what a pleasure that was, not to mention, I was to pay for my freedom, not pass on the cost to my ex!

I cannot remember a time when I felt more like a Jewish Woman of History. My shame was great, my failure exposed. I felt the foreboding of the woman of literature that wore a scarlet letter. My heart hurt.

I was excused from the room and I found myself teary eyed and in the foyer. As I walked to the door, another woman entered. She took one look at me and said, "What was it like? Was it awful?"

"It was very strange," I answered, holding back my tears so as not to scare her.

I walked into the dark night, free to make a new life. Still, I was very sad that what I thought would be a lifetime of goodness failed. How could a life together with such promise be so miserable? Our parents lived one house away from each other. My parents sat behind Gene's parents in our synagogue. Eugene went to college with my eldest first cousin. We had two beautiful sons. The sadness overwhelmed me as I drove home, tears falling down my cheeks and reviewing the ancient ceremony that cast me out of a family. There is simply no easy way to translate the feeling.

Harry & his parents

So Much Hope

Becoming a family
Harry's daughters
Stacey and Sheila

AS TIME GOES BY

With the optimism of Alice in Wonderland,
I began the next 23 years thinking I was going to be treated like I lived in a fairy tale, finally being able to take a deep breath and live the life I dreamed about for years.

Harry was older, a gentleman with that European savoir-faire, a true bon-vivant and every one was "Wild about Harry."

In earlier chapters, I shared how things began and there was no reason not to believe it was a sign of things to come. Obviously, any relationship I had with reality was not in my wheelhouse.

Sorry if I gave you any indication that the glass slipper was just my size and life at the palace was all I hoped it would be.

Before I realized it was happening, Harry became larger than life in my world. Everyone adored him, women told me how lucky I was to meet him. My family treated him like he walked on water. As tradition dictates, of course, I repeated the training that was legendary to every Jewish wife and soon I found myself in the same place that was as familiar as watching a rerun of "Yoo-Hoo, Mrs. Goldberg" for the fifteenth time.

As in many marriages, I could regale you with stories that would invoke laughter and tears. However, this memoir is my story. I spent twenty-three years with Harry to keep a promise to myself. When I met him and heard his story of life as a golden child then, totally disrupting his life at thirteen, to escape the nightmare of the Holocaust, I was shocked. Arriving in Shanghai, Harry's mother passing away the first year was another blow. I promised myself that I would make sure the next third of his life would be filled with as much joy as I could provide.

For the first seven years, I excused careless behavior feeling that the Holocaust years caused issues, like losing his mom at thirteen so that she didn't have time to teach him what he needed to know about women and his dad's inability to cope with the life transition. I believed that until I couldn't believe it anymore.

In our years, I learned that how I knew him was exactly the same as everyone else knew him. After the usual pleasantries, there was nothing to follow. It will be a surprise (maybe not) that we never had a conversation. If I called the store, when my car was stuck on the freeway, at the sound of my voice I had a rundown of what he had done to that point in the day. I learned quickly not to ask for help but take care of it myself.

Years passed by and I remained invisible. I worked in the store, studied and performed with a dance group, continued to do volunteer work, peeking out of the corner of my green velvet pea pod with yearning. That is, until Harry's heart surgery, when caregiving became an added attraction.

Fast forward, as Napa went through another transition, we closed the Napa store and moved to Sacramento. It was good for me to be with my children and dear friends. Being back in Sacramento was like the feeling one has when they put on their fleece lined, well broken in favorite slippers. I continued my volunteer activities and my dancing. Life continued in much the same way and then Cancer hit. To even explain that exercise in painful experiences, I put on my caregiver attitude once again and proud to say with an eighteen-month diagnosis, I kept him going for five years.

I kept my promise to myself. I provided a life for Harry that kept him safe, supported and content. While he could not express himself throughout our marriage, he left a letter in a plastic container that I found when he passed away. It said "Read after" and I did. I also shared it at his two Shiva minyanim with family and friends. It was my reminder to all that one should not wait until they are gone to say "I love you." It needs to be said often to those you cherish.

That is when I learned that Fairy Tales are what they are, make believe.

Mr. H Luggage updated
name for Napa

Right on First
Street in Napa

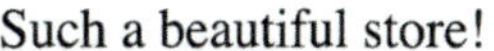

Such a beautiful store!

Back to work
after my dance troop performance

CONCLUSION

"Writing is a socially acceptable form of getting naked in public."

Paulo Choelho

THE GREAT TOILET PAPER CAPER

Bringing you into today's reality,
I will pause in my writing to share the current situation.

It is April 20, 2020, the age of the COVID-19 pandemic.
The time that the world entered the Twilight Zone. When we all began to live in some science fiction movie, starring the world.

It is the most frightening situation I could have imagined in my lifetime or any other person's lifetime. Yet, here we are practicing a mandated Shelter in Place or the acronym SIP. Our normal (whatever normal life means) everyday errands, chores, meetings, job or school just stopped with one court order. We have all been in our homes for almost two months. You only have to check on your computer to research the details.

I have spent days listening to politicians with their mixed messages, physicians with truth as much as they know about this mysterious plague, evening pundits, comedians making fun and doomsday folks frightening us as our heads spin with confusion.

I believe I am grateful for mobile phones, computers and other electronic devices, but am I? Yes, we can get the latest news, communicate with the outside world and feel some type of connection. My basic belief is that with all the technology of today our future could be living in caves and being in touch by gadgets. Okay, a generational attitude.

"When was the last time," I ask curiously, "you went to a restaurant, public gathering, coffee shop or witnessed a family of four at the next table sitting but everyone is on their phone?" The trend of the future.

Which leads me to the next question, how will young people date and marry? They don't know how to have a one-on-one conversation! I actually went to dinner at my niece's home and she texted her daughter, who was in her bedroom, to come to the dinner table. Really!

Today, I am thankful for the tools to stay in touch, however, awkward it may be, I want to share my humorous observations about this history making event.

As word of the world pandemic started to spread throughout the United States, fear set in and what do you suppose was the first thing that people did? Yes, it is true, they purchased toilet paper in huge quantities. Let me advise you that the Covid-19 illness was a respiratory related illness. It was droplets of infected matter that came through a cough or sneeze. Also, touching a table top or counter that might have active droplets. It didn't require toilet paper for other than regular use. However, every store was out of paper goods of all kinds. Some purchased in fear of not having enough and others decided to hoard it and go on an auction site and sell it for many times the normal cost. Those "not so bright" scammers were arrested and the last laugh was that their stash was not returnable!

Another situation that caused me to chuckle was the psychological effect that the SIP order caused as cabin fever, depression and social challenges set in.

I spent years listening to my friends and acquaintances say, "If I didn't have to work, I could get so much done at home." Or, "What I wouldn't give to be able to sleep in or just stay home and do nothing." I have never heard so much whining about having to stay home. Guess it is better when it is by choice and not very acceptable when it is ordered. After all, we live in the land of the free, not court ordered lock downs!!!

All I hear is how difficult it is to be home. Can you just imagine a Norman Rockwell picture showing the family gathered around the dinner table, mom in her apron serving the delicious pot roast with the aroma of potatoes and vegetables wafting through the house causing hunger pangs. The smiles on the faces of the children when dinner is served and after dinner, the father reading a book to the children gathered at his feet, totally enthralled with the story? Imagine parents and children having time for more than a "how was your day, have you finished your homework?" Parents exhausted from work, driving to volleyball or football games, trying to get dinner on the table, only to have dinner be carried to their rooms or in front of a television on a tray. Imagine time to get to know each other once again rather than ships passing in the night without a clue what is in each other's heart. What an opportunity to share, as people have not been able to do in many years.

Then there are the hysterical jokes and comedy sketches that appear on your computer all day. Like the husband and wife that worked out every day and were in wonderful shapes prior to the pandemic. They are standing in their foyer sharing the fact that once they could get in the door but after months of SIP, they were not able to get out of the door when the emergency was over because of their weight gain. Or the Broadway star and his rousing version of "Just a spoonful of Clorox makes the Temperature go down" after our current President of the United States in his very scary distortions stated "Perhaps you medical folks should think about injecting disinfectants into people since Clorox and other similar products kill the virus." I guess I don't have to describe the amount of clean-up (and I don't mean with detergents) the medical world, health advisers and media had to do to warn people not to even think about it! He was quite impressed with his genius and thought he could teach the medical world a few things. I believe he would be much better at reality television with his catch phrase "You're fired." If only we had the power to do that to politicians that have lost their sense of reality.

And now for the funny part. Allow me to share some of the most amusing repartee that has kept me home and laughing:

Two dogs sitting together. "Mom, why are humans wearing muzzles?"

"Honey, they are too dumb to learn 'sit' and 'stay'."

Commercials in 2030 will be like: Were you or someone you know overly exposed to hand sanitizer, Lysol or bleach during the 2020 Coronavirus pandemic? If so, you may be eligible for compensation.

There is nothing like a little tomato soup to soothe the soul. Even if it is cold, over ice, with a stalk of celery and, get ready, VODKA.

This quarantine made me realize I have no hobbies besides going out to eat and spending money.

I finally understand why dogs get so excited when they see an open door.

Quarantine has turned us all into dogs. We roam the house all day looking for food. We are told "NO" if we get too close to strangers. And, we get really excited about car rides.

In 8 weeks, 88% of blondes will disappear from the Earth.

Anyone else's car getting 3 weeks to the gallon at the moment?

Watch your local movie theater for the soon to be released epic "2020" written by: Stephen King and directed by Quentin Tarantino.

I've spent two weeks hanging out with myself and I apologize to every person that I have spent time with over the years.

If you thought toilet paper was crazy…just wait until 300 million people all want a haircut appointment at the same time.

Until further notice the days of the week are now called, Thisday, Thatday, Otherday, Today and Next day.

We will pause now for laughter recovery and get back to my story.

As for me, I am having quite an experience being home. I never thought I could enjoy my home so much. Especially with Chelsea, my darling poodle girl. She doesn't complain, argue or make any demands. She loves me in spite of my shortcomings and doesn't mind being spoiled rotten by me.

To broaden the scope of my world from inside, I moved my desk from facing a wall into the window of my upstairs den. I look out at the most beautiful trees, swaying as though they were hula dancing to the strains of "The Hawaiian Love" song. Under the trees on my patio the magnificent, brilliant pink, China Doll roses are watching the show, purple flowering bushes moving like hula skirts. The sun is shining, people are strolling, riding bikes, some masked, some not. I am watching the world coping and having hope; following the guidelines and showing gratitude for what is, not what is missing.

I have experienced several major historical events in my lifetime, like the Kennedy assassination, New York on 9/11 like it was a bad action movie, and other events. A worldwide plague, never in my radar. Total confusion in the medical community, messages to incite fear and worry with so many unanswered questions. However, human beings are survivors and courageous. Most are following the recommendations and staying put. The curve is starting to flatten. We are told that the hunt for a vaccine to beat this deadly virus will take up to eighteen months to be ready for us. Perhaps it will happen sooner.

Life is a beautiful thing however we choose to live it. I once was asked if I had a choice between love, money, health and success, what would be my first choice? Of course, it was health, without our health we are unable to have any of the other things.

If you want to find me in the future, I will be here in my home, being grateful, praying for an end to this plague along with more love and understanding for others; No matter their religion, skin tone, sexual orientation, country of origin or any other prejudice that we have experienced in the past.

A new day, a new appreciation, a chance to love all and be loved in return. Perhaps we will end this uncertain time with a kind spirit, a more loving heart and a newly cultivated sense of humor.

LIKE THE SAND IN THE HOURGLASS

So go the days of our lives. (A perfect introduction into a soap opera!) Joking aside, it is well past time to get to the core of this memoir.

While some are lucky enough to find themselves early in their life, others of us move through our lives with the gathered data we received as children. We were fulfilling the lifestyle that we were taught and we simply repeated it year after year. We travel our path, make what we feel are good choices, ignore the red flags and, sooner or later, we get the big bang.

Now, let me step back a bit and bring you up to date on the circumstances that brought about the transition that I will share with you. Even after Harry's cancer diagnosis, I kept up with all my volunteer projects, community obligations and full-time care of appointments and treatments for him. Why not? It was "Superwoman" in action. I didn't know anything else but to have a plate overflowing, so I volunteered to run the major fundraiser of the year for my synagogue. I desperately needed to have a long-term project so that I would have a reason to get up and out each day when Harry was no longer with us. I could sense we were getting very close. close.

Now I had two major projects to juggle while caregiving. Lucky for me, I had a wonderful woman, Api, join me during Harry's last months. It was such a relief, after more than four years, to have some help. I could actually sleep at night without one ear tuned in at all times. On Saturday morning, September 5, 2015 at five in the morning, I awakened to a silence in the house that was deafening. I raced upstairs and found Harry had passed away in what appeared to have been only minutes before I found him.

While I hesitate to use the word relief because it sounds so calloused, there is a certain feeling that takes over, especially as a caregiver, when a loved one finally is over such a terrible illness. Watching the suffering is so difficult for the family but letting go is agonizing. I must make a confession. When Harry was diagnosed, I prayed every day that he would be pain free.

Every doctor would ask Harry, “What is your pain level using 1-10?”

Each response from Harry was, “I am not having any pain.”

While I was grateful for his response, it was his first shot of morphine that allowed me to see his face relax and I knew that he didn’t acknowledge the pain. Was it an answer to my prayers? Or, was it an automatic response from a Holocaust survivor that would not let himself recognize pain? Here is my confession: on the Friday before he passed, I had my Rabbi come to our home to give Harry the Vidui blessing (more familiar to others as last rites). When the Rabbi left, I changed my prayers from pain-free to please take him out of his misery and give him peace. Thus, my discovery on Saturday morning (Shabbat) that he was gone. To this day, my son still asks me how I decided to have the Rabbi come to the house on that Friday. I cannot give him an answer. I do not have a clue why I called the Rabbi but I guess my intuition kicked in or my higher spirit danced in my atmosphere.

Following the customary rituals of Jewish burial, the next days were filled with the funeral, burial and Shiva minyanim. I was glad that I had the Gala to return to planning and I moved forward at warp speed. No time for tears or grieving in my world. Just a mad rush to keep doing what was required, but by whom? Wasn’t it just more of the same, being onstage at all times? Don’t show weakness. Always be a lady. Don’t make people uncomfortable because they don’t know what to say to you anyway. Each day went by with my public face on and rushing home to cover up in my welcoming green velvet pea pod. There I could just hide from reality and pretend that I was just doing what I was supposed to do, be content with the status quo. Don’t make demands, show weakness or be a burden to others.

The result of the big fundraiser, a great success. Mosaic Law had never had such a wonderful gala. The place was packed, the Rabbi was thrilled and we netted $107,000. A great job with much help from my friends. Now that the event was over, where was I planning to hide next?

Of course, it was with the Jewish Federation of the Sacramento Region. I was asked to step away from the Campaign and take the position of President. I had the time, experience and desire to lead this worthwhile endeavor but I needed time to think about it. While waiting to make my decision, which I ended up accepting, the Executive Director, Associate/ Communications Director, PJ Library associate, Social Worker and Campaign associate all resigned. Each person had a legitimate reason to move on, I just didn't expect they would do it all at once. It was my good fortune to have Elissa, Associate/Communications Director stay until she reached the day she was scheduled to make Aliyah (a move to Israel). We had three months to run the Federation and keep the doors open.

Our search for staff replacements went on and I became a volunteer director of my favorite non-profit organization. There we were, Adelita, our Office manager and me. We were able to hire a very qualified Social Worker, Rebecca and a creative, people person, Rikki, for our PJ Program (a monthly delivery of books focused on Judaism and moral values for children). Thus began our weekly office meetings and onward and upward direction for the JFSR*.

I found my new place to hide. What could be better than overseeing the entire community needs? It was made to order for a person like me, no matter how old I was. I couldn't understand that my needs and wants were not going to be met by the outside world. Hard to believe how long it can take to recognize that you have a problem. I sorely needed self-care. That unknown commodity that women of my generation were never taught. But I digress as I bring you along on my path of discovery.

I had an all-consuming purpose. I could continue to carry on the facade. It simply couldn't last forever, could it?

*Jewish Federation of the Sacramento Region

WHISTLE WHILE YOU WORK

It was simply perfect to have obligated myself to so many organizations that there just wasn't time for me to waste grieving.

I felt that it was important to keep moving so I increased the time for keeping busy by miles. Now I was busier than the Road Runner.

I thought that being the chairperson for the Federation was a perfect fit. I could volunteer 24/7, with all my years of experience, at my favorite organization. What better way is there to pay it forward than to devote all my time to social services? Perhaps, I should have taken a good look at myself and realized that to be successful, it was necessary to embrace some type of self-care. That was not something in my vocabulary, nor was it something I had the desire to even define. Being on overload was a comfort level. Smile and keep moving, that way no one could get too close or know me too well.

At one time, my doctor recommended that I see a Behavior Therapist. I decided to try it and there I learned that I had no concept about being centered. I was either all in or all out!

I had eating issues and when the therapist asked if I had eaten that day, my answer was no.

"What do you usually have for breakfast?" she asked.

"Oh, I like to fix a smoothie filled with all types of fruit, a bit of yogurt and my bits and pieces of banana, '' I answered.

"Why didn't you make a smoothie this morning?" she inquired.

"I was in too much of a hurry," I replied. "By the time I get out the blender, get the ingredients ready, blend it and wash the blender, I am running even later. I don't have that kind of time to waste."

"Do you actually have any idea exactly how long it takes?" the therapist queried. "Why not time it this week and when you come back, you can tell me how much time it actually takes to fix a smoothie?"

Now that was a challenge for me. I couldn't wait to test it and get back to her and tell her the ten or fifteen minutes that it takes. The day before the next appointment, I made sure to fix a smoothie and prove my point. It is no surprise to you but it certainly was to me. I believe it was less than four minutes to get it all done and I could see myself crawling into my next meeting with the therapist and having to confess my ignorance.

However, that lesson was not a keeper and before long, I was way off center again. Much to my dismay, the wonderful behavior modification therapist announced her retirement and I didn't have enough time with her to change my ways.

Leading the Jewish Federation as Chairman of the Board was the best job of my volunteer career. My world expanded as a result of my position. I had access to the entire community of nonprofits. I attended many interfaith events and met leaders from every community. I was able to be on the speaker's podium with clergy, civic leaders, and law enforcement leaders. I was included in holiday celebrations, memorials and community events along with leaders from the greater Sacramento area. My days were filled with our core Jewish value of TikKun Olam (the repair of the world). At long last, I was fulfilling my duty to perform 613 mitzvot (acts of good deeds), a directive from the Torah (our holy book).

I finally found the perfect hiding place out in plain sight. It was like a perpetual movie set. Smile, solve problems, say and do what I thought was the right and most diplomatic way to do things. It consumed my every waking moment and those middle of the night hours when I worried that I had missed doing something that day. I hired an Executive Director that I thought would take right over and build our organization into a power house. The resume was perfect, the personality and looks simply charming and I thought we were ready to set the world on fire. Funny thing about reality, it can hit you over the head with a baseball bat. When you ignore the red flags, for sure the Big Bang will get you when you are not paying attention. And I was just not paying attention!

THE SKY WAS FALLING

In my world of make believe, I was loving every minute of my job at Federation. Everything was so meaningful and alive. I kept the doors open and I vowed to rebuild the Federation as I dreamed it could be. Am I the eternal optimist or do I perpetually live in a fantasy world? I was soon to find out.

Sacramento is a very unique community. It is known for the diversity and connection of the community. However, as the state capital of California, it is on the bottom of the scale for fundraising. The bar is set very low in all areas of the community and all nonprofits are looking for much needed funding.

I took our recently hired Executive Director to every event in town; Introduced him at every venue in our community. Made sure he was visible at our congregations, often being invited to the bimah (pulpit) to introduce himself. We had meetings with community leaders and made sure that he had our community history as he met all the major leaders. I worked with him each and every day, either in person or by phone. I developed ideas and took them to him to see if he wanted the Federation to create them. We worked as a team, presented together and in my fantasy world, I thought it was Superman and Lois Lane, Batman and Robin or Fred and Ginger.

Slowly, I started to sense that something was off. The staff was polite but standoffish, very much different from usual smiles and hugs. In the office, things started to have a very different tint to the canvas. I began to question myself and it interrupted my path of progress.

When or why things changed, it doesn't matter. Explaining the progression of the disintegrating pattern, not necessary. It doesn't really matter except that it started to cause me anxiety. I couldn't get a bead on the core problem. Did I question the circumstances? Of course not. I was always the culprit and while I recognized that something was not right, I could only account for my behavior.

Being the person with a well-crafted facade, I tried so hard to carry on as normal. Each day, I ran faster, worked harder, tried to make things right and chastised myself for doing something I didn't realize I did. And then the confusion took hold of me and I found I was suffering. Then the sky did fall.

It was a Saturday afternoon. I came home from a Mah Jongg game, hot, tired, and more than that, beyond exhaustion. Of course, I was aware of that. All I knew was to keep occupied and not falter. I went upstairs to my office, started to say something to my dog and the words came out all funny. I could not put a sentence together; I could not put the words in order. I didn't know what was happening, I only knew I was beyond tense and scared that I was having a stroke. Imagine how anxiety can manifest itself in such a scary way.

I raced to my car and drove to the Urgent Care three blocks away. How dumb was that to get into a car and drive? Luckily, the office was just closing. I begged the man closing up to take my vitals and tell me if I was in trouble.

He took my temperature, blood pressure and heart rate.

Then advised me, "You seem okay but it might be a good idea to call your doctor's office and see what they say."

It was after five on Saturday, I got home and called since my doctor's office has a nurse on call 24/7. After hearing my story, the on-call nurse suggested that I go to the emergency room just to double check.

It is good to note that this was during the terrible flu epidemic of 2017. I called my pet sitter to come as soon as she could and then made another call.

I called my dear friend and neighbor, with a huge lump in my throat asked, "I need to go to the emergency room. Can I pick you up on the way so that I am not alone?"

"Absolutely not," she said, "I will pick you up and you are not to drive yourself."

She dropped me at the door of the hospital and went to find a parking spot. I entered what looked like a war zone. People in all states of illness were filling the entire room. Coughing, sneezing, blowing and more, I was horrified. What was I doing here? I checked in at the desk and thankfully, they had prepared for me so that I was not in the middle of "Germville," nor was I in the hallway. Lucky for me, they found what might have been a utility closet at one time that fortunately had a bathroom. I was grateful for the restroom but not so happy with the slab of wood that was being used for a bed.

A long story short, I was given an unending series of tests, kept in my utility room while the staff told me that they did not, and would not have, a room available for me. I was tended to by a young doctor that I couldn't believe was a doctor. She had long brown hair, the adorable face of a twelve-year-old girl and only needed a bundle of colored balloons in one hand and cotton candy in the other to complete the picture. At that point, with tests all negative, I asked to be released so that I could go home. My wish was granted. However, something was triggering my nervousness and anxiety. Things just didn't seem to be settling down and I knew I was in trouble.

At home, I began a very difficult week. First, the young doctor prescribed a very large increase in one of my medications that I seriously considered ignoring since this was done without consulting my personal physician. Being an orderly, follow directions type, even in doubt, I took the pills as directed. Two hours later, I was on the floor writhing in pain from an overdose that was too much for my frame. I suffered all night and could not wait to speak to my doctor at a decent hour in the morning.

Without an entire story, I recovered from the medication when my doctor put me back on the regular dosage. Then I found out that my coughing and congestion was a virus that I picked up at the hospital. It was the week that was.

By now, knowing that I didn't have a stroke or heart issue, I was simply experiencing panic and anxiety attacks on a regular basis. I began to take every holistic anti-anxiety potion on the market.You name it, I tried it. Still, the attacks came like clockwork and I felt more frightened every day.

It was a Sunday morning when an attack hit that was all I could take. I called my pharmacist, no answer. Then a pharmacist friend, no answer and, in desperation, I called my neighbor, Sue. She is a social worker and we were casual acquaintances at the time. I was so desperate that I decided to impose and call her. Lucky for me she was home. Sue had shoulder surgery and was recovering with her arm in a sling.

With a choked voice, I said between gasps, "I am having terrible anxiety attacks and am terrified. Forgive me for interrupting you on a Sunday but I am so frightened."

Surprisingly, Sue sweetly replied, "I was sitting at home feeling sorry for myself because I was unable to see my clients during my recovery from shoulder surgery. When you called, I was praying that God would find some useful purpose for me during my convalescence. Then you called and I knew He answered my prayers."

Sue stayed with me until I felt better and informed me that she shared an office with a therapist that specializes in Post Traumatic Stress issues. She sent me the phone number and first thing Monday morning I called and left a message. Then, I sat by the phone waiting to hear from what I hoped would be a miracle worker.

Several days passed and I was like a cat on a hot tin roof waiting to get a call back. At long last, the phone rang, I saw the name on the call alert.

I grabbed the phone and answered, "Oh, is it my angel? Thank goodness you have called."

Nancy responded with, "I had a cancellation this afternoon. Can you be here by 2:45pm?"

"Absolutely," I replied, "I can't believe it. It is a miracle."

That was January, 2018. What a start to a new year. I never imagined it would be the beginning of freedom. I felt the lock on the cage jiggle.

BREAKING NEWS

It is November 2020, and this is truly history.

The presidential election has taken place and, to date, the 45th President of the United States of America Donald J. Trump has lost the race. He is refusing to concede to President Elect, Joseph Biden.

Mr. Trump has stayed secluded unless absolutely necessary and he has refused to show any type of leadership to the country.. He will not accept his loss, has demanded recounts in several states and claims that the election is a fraud. He believes he will be declared the winner and begin his second term on January 20, 2021.The country is gripped with anxiety.

The country is in turmoil as the pandemic numbers continue to climb, while believing that we would be resuming our usual life, we are on the brink of a country-wide shutdown again.

This is an historical time for us. Buy books now to have in your library for your children and grandchildren since you will have amazing stories to share with them. Books are coming out daily from those involved in Washington, D.C. We have no idea what the outcome will be. However, it was clear from the start that Mr. Trump was in the White House permanently. It will take the National Guard dragging him out kicking and screaming at the end of four years, if he lasts that long.

But enough about world history, let's get back to my story.

KEEPER OF THE KEY

What a cluster of raw emotion to be sitting in a strange building waiting to see the person whom you hope will save you from the wrong path you have taken. Your anxiety is running rampant and your brain is questioning what in the world you are doing in this place and when you lost control of your life.

A vintage older home on I Street, currently used as office space, was the location of the therapist's office. I walked up the entry steps and entered what I can only assume was the large entry hall. There were no instructions anywhere about signing in and one client was sitting in a chair waiting. We nodded at each other in the way that clients do when our instinct is to say that you are not a client but dropping off a letter for a friend. As I moved across the room, I noticed a little alcove with bench seating and some magazines. I tucked myself away in the little section and figured that Nancy would come looking for me as I nonchalantly pretended to be reading.

Shortly thereafter, Nancy appeared and invited me into her office. We exchanged pleasantries and the entire time my head was screaming, *save me. Where do we begin and does this ever end?*

I could see that Nancy was a straight to the point person and was not spending the day on her couch pondering how many more years of this until retirement. No nonsense, she got right to it.

I began to talk about the episodes I was experiencing and all the holistic products I had purchased from the health food store. The many books I was reading and my effort to try and meditate.

With the strength of a roaring lion, Nancy replied, "Forget about all those things. You are so ill that you are going to need real medication to help you and you won't be through with me until August."

I reacted with my usual and appropriate self, trying to act out my control and ability to function no matter what. All the time praying that I had found a place where the painful pretense and stoicism could finally stop. Did I have what it takes to move forward or am I going to smile at the end of the session, extend a polite thanks and race home at 65 mph? I was hoping to get home, seek out my velvet hideaway and forget trying to fix it. I decided to trust Nancy instead of myself. It turned out to be one of the best decisions of my life.

Our time together provided the opportunity for me to share my secrets and Nancy, being a long- time feminist, gave me permission to explore and accept all the qualities that I had kept hidden my entire life. My green velvet pea pod, where I hid out for so long, was starting to come apart at the seams - but I was starting to shed my cocoon.

Yes, I found a haven to repair my heart and soul. My tool box was almost filled with everything to heal. Until July hit, when Nancy shared with me the diagnosis of an illness that would require her to close her practice to tend to her needs.

Stricken with the news of her illness, my first instinct was to take care of her. Give back what I had been taking from her for nine months. Then there is Nancy, the no nonsense, face life, believe, be vulnerable, fight for yourself and win the battle. I would try to find an appropriate way to fulfill my need to help.

By this time, Nancy and I developed a very healthy bond. I had such respect for her and her style of practice. She, in turn, respected me and stated that she didn't know anyone else who lived the way I did. My favorite comment from Nancy, that I will never forget:

"You know, Carol," she said with love and humor, "I like it when you are my last client. It always makes my day worthwhile and I enjoy our sessions so much."

Nancy could never imagine the tremendous respect and gratitude for all she taught me at the most important time of my life. Without her, my transition, self-care and awareness would never have happened. Have I got it all down pat? No way. I am a butterfly still getting used to her wings. Would another year of Nancy's wisdom help me even more? Of course, but we all know that she gave me everything I needed to work with and the rest was up to me.

With that knowledge, I began to hear the slow rattle of the large brass lock that kept me caged for so long. I could just feel that the key was close by. I was closer than ever to finding freedom.

Nancy Grant, LCSW

May 3, 1953 - April 15, 2022

Nancy Grant passed peacefully at her home in Albany on Good Friday. Nancy was surrounded by her loving husband, Craig of 39 years and her four children. Nancy was born at Marin General Hospital and grew up in San Rafael, California. She was a West End kid, attending West End Elementary, Davidson Junior High, and graduating from San Rafael High in 1971. Nancy was a life-long defender and advocate for women's rights. She learned early on to question authority. As a 7th grader she went toe to toe with the principal of Davidson Junior High who tried to suspend her for wearing shorts instead of dress to a Saturday school function. She loved animals deeply, continuing her rebellious streak in high school by freeing soon-to-be-dissected frogs from Mr. Lack's biology class. Twice! Later in life, she would be fired from her position as executive director of the Davis Rape Crisis Center for reading the penal code to the Yolo County Sheriff. She did not suffer fools.

A 1975 graduate of Pitzer College, Nancy continued her education and received a Master of Science degree in Social Work from Sacramento State University in 1983. She was a gifted and caring therapist. As a mental health practitioner in private practice for nearly 40 years, Nancy always saw who people could be in their best selves. She connected with clients deeply, helping literally hundreds of people of all socioeconomic backgrounds in both Redding and Sacramento. Nancy particularly loved working with teens and young adults. She specialized in helping people recover from trauma and was an early adopter and skilled practitioner of Eye Movement Desensitization and Reprocessing therapy. Near the end of her career, she was excited by the development of the "flash EMDR" technique and recognized its potential to help a myriad of people, from pandemic survivors to war veterans.

Nancy and Craig were childhood friends who reconnected at their 10-year high school reunion, where they learned they both lived in Sacramento. They were married a year later in Grand Marais, MN. After five happy years of marriage, Nancy informed Craig that it was time for children (they had never discussed kids prior to the clock ticking over). They had two wonderful children, Samantha and Jeff, both born in Sacramento. After moving to Redding, Nancy and Craig became foster parents to Nikki McGovern, and later, her brother, Chris McGovern. Both kids became, and remain, integral parts of the family. Nancy often said adopting Nikki and Chris was the best thing that ever happened to our family.

Nancy is pre-deceased by her parents, Leslie Alan Grant and Wilma (Read) Grant of San Rafael. She is survived by her husband Craig Martz and their four children, Chris McGovern, Nikki (McGovern) Cuffe, Samantha Martz Cohen and Jeff Martz, as well as four grandchildren, Deja McGovern Renk, Colton Harvey, Lev Cohen, and Mira Cohen. A celebration of life was held at her daughter's home in Marin.

166

THERAPY - NOT FOR THE FAINT OF HEART

At the mere mention of the word therapy, people tend to turn a very unusual shade of beige.

It feels like finding yourself going through an amusement park in a very dark tunnel and strange monsters keep popping out and scaring you.

When all is said and done, an average client is thrilled with the result. It is getting there that is difficult. You are not sure you believe what you are hearing, you are always careful that you don't look bad, leery of telling all and being judged.

Take it from me, it is like winning the lottery if you have the guts to make the commitment and push forward.

The beginning for me was in January of 2018. As I had referenced in a prior chapter, I was having serious panic attacks diagnosed as exhaustion. Nancy stated that I would be needing help until, at least, August. That gave me plenty of time to sandbag and not get right to it. I knew I was really a mess. Always worried, sometimes feeling so alone, filled with anxiety and pretending to be fine. I couldn't wait to get to my appointment but started clamming up the minute I was walking up the stairs to the office.

Nancy, my therapist, made me understand that the first act of my therapy session was to strike the word "STOIC' from my vocabulary. Here I thought it was a badge of honor to not show tears or emotion, simply greet and support others. I could show how beautifully I could handle the crisis at hand without putting an onus on others. What a ridiculous thing that is to try and do. Your inside organs are at war with each other, the noise in your head is louder than a brass band and you are smiling. How is that for a mixed message to your brain? Brain-tease is one subject that I could earn an A+ in during my facade of calm, cool and composed. The dreaded three C's! It was a comfort zone to chastise myself after everything I did with all the could, would and should things that would have made it better.

I could hear my mother's voice chanting, "you are wrong."

Nancy was a warrior and she had no intention of letting me get away with dragging my feet for long. As in past therapy experiences, I had to tell my history from birth to present. Nancy stayed in the present and worked with my real time concerns. How my issues came about would be revealed at some point in my future sessions.

Nancy had a marvelous way of not allowing me to demean myself or beat myself with a large stick. Her goal was to get me to accept myself. She gave me permission to release my misconceptions and critique of everything I said and did. At long last I realized that, at some point, I was going to unlock the cage. Even if the electronic device to locate the key was not on my key fob, instinct told me that it was hidden somewhere in that office. I began to feel so hopeful.

"You were born ten years too soon, "Nancy would say, "You were a feminist long before it was fashionable to be recognized as one."

I will admit that often times my thoughts would focus on when I didn't fit in or said the wrong thing that made other women look at me like I was from Mars. As a child, no matter how many colors of dotted Swiss dresses with lace pinafore, or large silk bows of every color and pattern were put in my hair, I still wanted to read another book or ask questions that would not be answered. Simply waved off like it was a joke and my misfit status took another hit.

Slowly my tool kit started to fill. It contained self-esteem, self-care, acceptance, refusal to be in toxic company, and a slow awareness that I may be okay, recognizing my gifts and blessings. Each week I would fight new awareness with old beliefs. Day by day, I would try to accept what Nancy was guiding me to believe.

You cannot imagine what it felt like to know that I didn't have to hide or be ashamed of being intelligent. No, not everyone in the world can do what I do! I believed if a loser like me could complete a project with success, so could any other average person. Only, I believed that "other person" could do it better. The mantra had played in my head for decades. I wanted to hide any skills and hang out in my faded green velvet pea pod. If I was the recipient of compliments but one criticism, that one criticism was my only take away.

However, week to week, as I started to question more, I began to hear all the statements. It was no longer selective listening. With utter disbelief, I listened and absorbed the dialogue of our sessions. Then it happened: I stood up to leave the office and had a vision in my head that the key had floated into the lock and the cage was opened. My heart jumped into my throat and I could feel a new beginning start to happen.

The golden cage was open for me if I could find the courage to move forward and not live as I had in the past. It is not easy to try and change the perceptions of a life time. Without Nancy, could I soar like a butterfly?

FOR RENT: A GILDED CAGE

How strange life can be at times.
I was finally blossoming into the new me.

What a shock it was to my comfort zone when Nancy informed me that she had been diagnosed with an illness that was going to require her to close her practice and retire.

Part of me had so much gratitude for all that she had given me, the other part wanted to embrace her and take care of her.

Two steps back, one step forward, I've got this!

"Nancy, I believe that I see a gold key on the top of your table," I blurted out during one of our last sessions, "I believe the lock on my cage may be open."

"How very funny," Nancy replied looking very confused, "I don't see a key. What are you talking about? Are you having illusions all of a sudden?"

"Really, Nancy," I responded with puzzlement, "it must be so, I thought I saw a key."

At that moment, I felt so silly. Of course, Nancy didn't see the key. It was my imagination acting out the fantasy of my pea pod hiding place, the golden key and my life in a cage. All my therapy was about finding that key. Why would I think Nancy would be in my fantasy of escapism when, in fact, she was the conduit for me to reach for the key and give myself the freedom that I longed to enjoy? Nancy, the puppet-master, miracle worker and guide.

Nancy and I had several sessions before she closed her practice. She planned to stay in touch with a few of her patients, including me. How I hoped that would happen and she would have a complete recovery and reopen her practice. That was not to be. Nancy's treatments consumed much of her time. Her family togetherness became her most important source of comfort. She eventually left the area and moved to San Francisco near her children to share time and support as she went through her care process and for family to give comfort to her husband.

Lucky for me, the short time spent with Nancy made an enormous impact on the way that I was living my life. Each week, my tool kit became filled with needs that would keep me on the road to a better way to live my life.

Nancy made very clear the generational conditions that dominated most of my choices. She worked to try and erase the negative thoughts and feelings that ran through my head like a broken record. Should, would, could and never enough. I could not see the positive things I did but could only evaluate on what I should/could have done better.

She stressed the rhetoric I was raised on could be abandoned; that I must follow, respect and do what was traditional in my background. She reminded me of my struggles about being born too early to acknowledge my feminist instincts. She destroyed my need to beat myself with a large stick for wanting to pursue something other than having a nice Jewish marriage and giving my parents perfect grandchildren. The fight may have been too much for me at that time before I was strong enough to reject what was expected of me, but she had me lay down the stick I beat myself with over this. While I didn't follow the path I wanted, my gifts are two very fine men that I was blessed to bring into this world and raise.

Nancy clearly pointed out the number of toxic individuals and situations I accepted like it was my job to right every wrong. She gave me permission to acknowledge my strong points that I tried so hard to hide. She was taking Humpty Dumpty apart and putting me back together as an accepting, forgiving person allowing myself to live the life that was given to me. I only had to answer to myself and that would take some work to get used to in my world.

I flew out of my self-imposed cage and slowly felt the joy of freedom to explore, experiment and learn the meaning of self-care. Like any other life addiction, I couldn't disconnect totally but I was much more conscious of my choices. I could recognize the difference between my needs and my habits. I was completely aware that it was now or never to become the free spirit I wanted to be. Yes, the same desire to make the world a better place was still a priority but, now, as an authentic person, not a performance that I felt was required. It was Tikkun Olam (repairing the world) in its true form. Remembering always that the opposite of Love is not hate, the opposite is fear. I had a life of fear while my heart always beat with love.

With transition to authenticity, fear was no longer in control of my life, keeping me caged. Stoic and accepting were not part of my vocabulary. I began to soar and it felt wonderful except for several crash landings. Now I could pick myself up, shake out my wings and fly away.

THE POODLE PARADE PLUS

It would not be possible to write anything about my life without introducing the parade of poodles that have shared their lives with me.

From my first black miniature poodle brought home when I was a teenager until this very day, as a senior citizen, my life has been enriched by my fur babies.

Many years have passed, I cannot remember the circumstances prior to the arrival of a beautiful, black, miniature poodle puppy that joined our home in San Francisco. Looking back, I cannot recall any discussion that indicated the family was thinking about a pet. Our home was quite elegant. Located in the outer Richmond district close to Sea Cliff, I couldn't imagine that my mother would allow a dog into her silk brocade embellished home decorated with the type of grand furniture and accouterments that filled a classic home in her generation. We were not allowed into the living room without being invited and dressed in best of the closet clothes. Our living room had sliding doors with glass panels which allowed us to look into the room but not enter without permission.

My most embedded memory of that room was the fireplace that was covered in a mirror finish that had a smoked design of white on each side. At Chanukah, the floor in front of the fireplace was filled with the single gifts of each member of the family to give out on their night. Remember, we celebrate each night of the eight-day holiday and receive one gift from the family member that lights the candle that evening. The night my father lit the candles was the only no-limit gift night. When we arrived downstairs in the morning when it was Daddy's turn, the floor was filled in front of the entire fireplace. He was the best gift-giver ever and we were spoiled. Our best rendition of a night visit from Hanukkah Claus.

Back to our dog stories. As a reminder, I was dancing at the time and I was asked to suggest a name for the puppy. I chose Tour jete (a ballet move) and that name was voted in by the family. Thus,Tour jete became the darling of our family and was the dedicated pet of Uncle Sam. Actually, I am not sure which one was more devoted.

Tour jete was followed by small black siblings, a boy and a girl that joined the homes of my sister and me. We were both living on the San Francisco Peninsula and I added Trinket to my family. Trinket's sister, Jolie, lived with Beverly's family. Shortly thereafter, I added a miniature white poodle we named Snoopy.

Without the entire poodle history, you would have no way of knowing that there was a constant parade of poodles throughout my life. Fast forward to when Carol met Harry.

At that time, I had wavered a bit and I decided to try different breeds, a Schnauzer named Priscilla Ann and a Yorkie named Randy. I tried to accept another breed but, truth be told, I was a dedicated poodle person. Priscilla Ann and Randy were fun pets but not poodles.

Also, don't faint, three cats had adopted me. Allow me to say that I was afraid of cats forever. Every time they curved their little paws and showed their claws, I wouldn't go near a cat for fear of getting scratched and, G_d forbid, Cat Scratch Fever. But they are fur babies too and it seems I had some type of invisible sign attached to my home that read "Abandoned Cats Welcome Here." I believe that I only purchased one cat in my life, the rest came to my door and announced that they wanted to live with me.

Thus, Binky came to me. Binky sat in front of my house for days and soon I left a bed on the porch and food for him. Binky was a gorgeous ebony feline with piercing deep green eyes. His name should have been King Ali Caht as he was the epitome of a regal Egyptian revered black cat. I still feared having him in the house until I couldn't fight my need to protect him.

One evening, a television reporter warned: "The temperature this evening is going to dip and there is a frost warning for tonight. Be sure to keep your animals inside."

That is the night Binky moved into the garage, soon to take over the back bedroom and he was officially named Binky. He was sweet and smart. Smart enough to win me over. In my research I learned that black cats are special. In Egypt, you were given a black cat as a spiritual gift. One never purchased a black cat and, when given, brings good luck. I learned to love cats and soon the inn was filled with Mittzi, Tiny Girl and Scooter.

When Harry met Carol and the dating began, I was informed by Harry that he only allowed his daughters to have one dog and his name was Oy Vey. Other than that, pets were not his thing. Boy, was he in the wrong place! As our long-distance relationship grew, we began to discuss getting married and I would be moving back to the Bay Area where Harry had his three luggage stores. Not surprisingly, Harry did not want to adopt five pets. Friends and family were constantly at me.

"Get rid of those animals," said a close friend raising her voice at me. "Don't you realize how lucky you are to find someone like Harry?"

I pondered, "Do I really need all this advice? Maybe I better think about it."

While having my nails done, I shared my dilemma with my manicurist. She mentioned that they were thinking about getting a dog for their daughters. We set up a time to bring Priscilla Ann to their home to meet the girls. I asked my sister to go with me and teary- eyed started to gather all Priscilla's possessions. I was sick to my stomach as we drove to the lady's home. Carrying Priscilla into the house was gut wrenching.

One of the little girls cried out, "Oh, what an ugly dog, get it away from me."

Poor Priscilla panicked and ran for the patio door. The father proceeded to open the door and out Prissy went without us knowing that an unfenced swimming pool was right outside of the door. Plop went Prissy right into the freezing pool on a cold winter night. I grabbed her, told Bev to grab Priscilla's things and we were out of there as fast as we could go.

With Harry coming up to Sacramento on the weekend, I was impatiently waiting. I couldn't wait for him to arrive so I could get my anger off my chest. Late afternoon he arrived and I was ready to state my case. As it happened, he arrived earlier than I expected and I was fresh out of the shower with my wet hair dripping down my face. I asked him to sit himself down as I had something to say.

"You seem so upset," queried Harry, as he looked at me with puzzlement. "Have I done something?"

"I don't know if you have or not," I snapped back. "I just know that I want to stay as your girlfriend only and will not even consider marrying you."

Panicked, Harry answered, "What is the matter? What has happened?"

"I had the worst time last night," I spit out. "I have absolutely no intention of giving up my pets for you. I have had them longer than I have known you and I trust them. I just don't know about you. I am not giving up my pets and that is that!"

With what appeared to be relief, Harry replied, "Okay, we will manage."

With that I answered, "Fine, then I may reconsider."

Thus, we married and had a menagerie. Each pet, at one time or another, sat on Harry's lap and tried to make friends with no result. Harry had only one observation.

"I always thought cats were all alike," he mused. "I am amazed by their different personalities."

Tiny Girl was the only one that never gave up on him and continued to sit on his lap during television time hoping he would finally pet her. She finally gave up too.

With time, my pets were lost one by one. I was trying to adjust to not having a poodle and I wasn't handling it well. One day when Harry and I were on the market buying for the store, we saw a woman with the tiniest dog walking in front of us. Both of us fell in love with the little dog and decided that the time was right to start looking around and see if we could find a replica of the adorable dog. I kept my cool but I was jumping out of my skin with excitement. The search was on and I started with a poodle breeder in Napa. She had a darling teacup girl that looked at me with that "please take me home" look in her eye. I just got cold feet and said I wanted to think about it. I have regretted that decision to this day.

I was reading the Napa Register one morning and saw an ad for three toy poodles available: Two brown and one black. I called the person with the ad and had quite an unpleasant experience.

"I own the luggage store in downtown Napa and I am calling to inquire about your ad for a toy poodle," I said. "Can you give me some information about them? Are they available to see and make a selection?"

She responded with unexpected anger. "I know about rich b___ches like you. You want to come and check out my house. You can just forget about it."

With that, she hung up and I was holding the phone in my hand wondering what the heck had happened. I could not stop thinking about her response but I just didn't want to try again.

Harry and I had a meeting to attend on the weekend and we left the store for several days and had our manager take care of the shop. When we checked on the store that evening, Sheryl shared some news with us.

"This afternoon, a big van pulled up in front of the store," Sheryl told us. "This tough looking woman walks in with the most adorable brown poodle puppy and asks to see you. I told her that you were out of town."

"Have one of them call me when they get back," she threw out as she walked away.

With some trepidation, I picked up the phone and called her. I asked her not to yell at me, but was the puppy still available? And that is how Mocha came to join our family.

My only regret is that I did not take the other brown puppy. Everyone wanted a dog like Mocha. Harry adored Mocha and finally enjoyed the benefit of becoming friends with a pet. He told everyone Mocha was his son. I was thrilled that he could outwardly show emotion.

Mocha took us from Napa, where he worked in the store in his security jacket, to retirement in Sacramento enjoying the good life sitting on Harry's lap. Mocha was such a comfort to Harry in the last stages of his illness. When Harry passed, I designed his headstone with a soccer ball in one corner, a royal flush in the other corner and Mocha's footprints all over the stone. Sadly, I lost Mocha in 2017 and that certainly ended an era for me.

Ghost sounds of Mocha came from all over my home and soon the emptiness was more than I could take. After much searching, I found my beloved Chelsea on Craig's List of all things. I wasn't sure how safe it was to buy a dog on Craig's List. One of my friends found the cutest Yorkie that way so I decided to give it a try.

I finally found an ad for a "Toy poodle": Three years old, salt & pepper, great disposition, loves toys and children. All shots $200. That should have been enough to scare me off. I sent a text asking the size of the poodle, if she could send a picture and where they were located. Answer: 9 lbs., picture was adorable and they were located in Red Bluff. After a conversation, we agreed to meet in Williams the following week and I gave no guarantee that I would take her. My dear friend, Lorraine, went with me. An odd fact, Chelsea was placed on Craig's List the day I buried Mocha. She was destined to be mine since she was on the list for two weeks. Trust me, if there had been a picture on the post, she would have been adopted the very first day by someone else.

At first sight, Peppa, as she was called then, was pulling on her leash and not the little poodle princess that I hoped for (not yet, anyway). I had a new blanket, treats and a toy in the car because I was going to take her no matter what. After all, she would be placed somewhere and better with me. I put her on my lap on her new blanket and she didn't make a sound the entire way home. I never thought any dog could be all that Mocha was to me but very quickly Chelsea (what kind of a name is Peppa!) captured my heart and that of every neighbor, friend, visitor or casual stroller. They could not resist her as she went to say hello, always carrying a different toy in her mouth. People would stop just to see what toy she was carrying that day.

Sadly, I had her for only a short time. I always thought that she was older than I was told and it proved to be true. At what I thought was only six years old, Chelsea developed kidney failure that took her from me within a month. The day she was to enter her final sleep, neighbors came by the house all morning to say goodbye to her. As I held her in my arms, wrapped in her favorite blanket, with a piece of red string from Israel tied to her ear (we wear red string to keep the bad spirits away), she took her final breath and my heart crumbled.

Lucky for me, Joel had moved back to Sacramento and he was able to take us to Bubbling Well Memorial Park in Napa where she was laid to rest with her seven brothers and sisters. Of course, dear friend, Lorraine took that last journey with us.

At this time of my life, I decided that perhaps I was better pet-less. I tried to understand what others told me about why they will never get another pet. Taking trips without concern for providing care for their pet, no feedings, walking, changing litter boxes, paying vet bills but they did not realize the loss of unconditional love each day that was making me so sad.

Weeks passed and as expected, I disliked being in such a quiet house. Ghost sounds, walking in without a greeting, nothing to take care of and no warm fur baby in my lap. Casually, I started to check the computer just to see if there was a purebred, female, teacup toy poodle for sale. What a rude awakening, there are few purebred poodles of any size. They are being inbred with every other breed possible. I believe the least expensive purebred I found was over five thousand dollars.

On with my search and it was fruitless. I tried every rescue, newspaper, friend and, of course, Craig's List. Nothing! I wondered if I had any poodle breeders listed on a very old email address that I rarely use any longer. I found two breeders. One was the lady that I didn't take that darling poodle from years ago. I decided to call her anyway. She asked my age and when I told her, she refused to sell me one of her dogs because I was too old. That certainly sent me to the mirror and a wrinkle remover application.

Next, I found Paradise Poodles. Paradise? Best I checked on the computer and there it was, Paradise Poodles, now in Olivehurst, Ca because of the wildfire that destroyed the town of Paradise a few years earlier. The breeder, Joan, was able to save seven poodles during the fire but lost her home, studio, kennel, mare and chickens. I was heartsick to hear her story. I asked if she had a female poodle that was no longer used for breeding that she wanted to sell. Since she was a standard poodle breeder, she only had one beautiful cocoa-colored standard and she was 45 pounds. Of course, at five feet, I could never handle her. Then she considered for a few minutes selling her own white, large miniature (an oxymoron) girl to me and letting her have a sweet rest of her life. She went on to tell me that her dog was eight years old and when she was spayed, they found several benign tumors in her stomach. How many red flags did I need? I thanked Joan and said I would think about it.

Several days later, I had a call from Joan. She explained that she had a policy about her poodles. If someone buys a dog from her, cannot keep it and does not have a family member or reliable source to raise that dog, it must be returned to Paradise Poodles. She went on to say that she had a woman and her husband choose a black miniature boy to add to their family. As the pandemic began, the woman called Joan and told her that they had decided to return the dog after two years. Then Joan never heard from her again. Some weeks before I called, Cooper (as he was known then) was returned. Not neutered, not well cared for and just left. Joan's explanation was that they lost their business during the pandemic and were moving out of state. As a thought, Joan wondered if I would like to meet Cooper.

Several years ago, I found a standard poodle for a dear friend of mine. Sharing my current poodle saga, Phyllis had accompanied me to all the end-of-life visits with Chelsea. Phyllis was the first friend to see Chelsea and she named her. She wanted to be part of a new pet for me and asked to drive with me to Olivehurst to see the available poodles.

The night before we went, I kept a small blanket in bed with me. I wanted to have my scent on something I might leave with a potential addition to my home. We arrived at Paradise Poodles, meeting Joan at her rustic new location. We drove down a dirt road and found the property. A modest house, a broken-down gate, barren land, a small cottage that Joan used for grooming and it was clear the toll that the Paradise fire had taken on this long established fine poodle breeder.

Joan was just finishing her grooming session with her white dog when we arrived. She put her white dog down and immediately we were joined by a stunning miniature black poodle. Obviously, the dog named Cooper. I walked over and sat on the step of Joan's house and the black dog came and sat down by my side. At first, I was a bit uncomfortable because he was so large. Chelsea was only nine pounds and Cooper was twenty five pounds. After our brief visit, I told Joan that I would think about it, tucked the Carol scented blanket in Cooper's bed and said our goodbyes.

I was conflicted for a few days because it was such a large dog. Let me mention that Cooper could have been a twin of my very first poodle, Tour jete. I called Joan soon after our visit and asked if she would deliver Cooper to me, with the blanket, so the transfer would be smooth. Joan planned on driving into Sacramento on Friday and was delighted to bring the dog to me.

I couldn't wait for him to arrive. Since the family across the street from me had a dog named Cooper, it was the final step to be able to change his name. For such a regal looking poodle, Cooper was definitely not the name for him. He was renamed "Sir Bentley" on his second day in my home. Lovingly called Ben or Benji. I wanted a bit of a Hebrew flavor to his name

Sir Bentley has been my precious fur baby since May 14, 2021. The bond was instant and I can almost believe that Mocha and Chelsea got together at the Rainbow Bridge and selected Bentley for me. Just when you think that you could never be blessed with another of G_d's gifts, a new fur baby arrives at your door. After all, isn't a dog simply G_d spelled backwards?

Bentley is as special as a pet can be. His eyes radiate with the love and gratitude that he feels for me and I return the same. We do everything together. The fact that he is so big gives me the feeling of a warm, soft, fluffy cuddle pillow that makes everything right with the world. A terrific trade-off for a pea green velvet pea pod.

Since Ben is only two years old, I wish for us a long and healthy life together. My prayers are that we end our beautiful love story at the same time.

My first poodle, a miniature black boy and the dog my parents would not let me keep.

The first of a trifecta Moocha

Snoopy and his litle sister Trinket

Tiny girl ran away from an unhappy home and found me.

My precious Binky passed away and I adopted Mitzi from a pet store. I had to have a black cat!

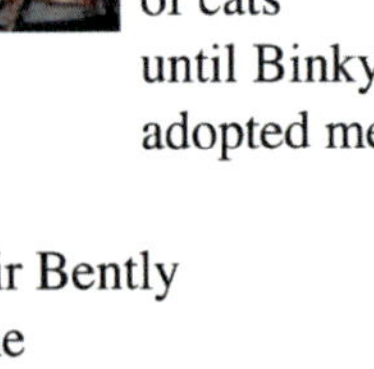

Terrified of cats until Binky adopted me

Priscilla Ann and her little brother Randy

Sir Bently the Magnificent

I think Scooter saw a "For Rent" sign on my home

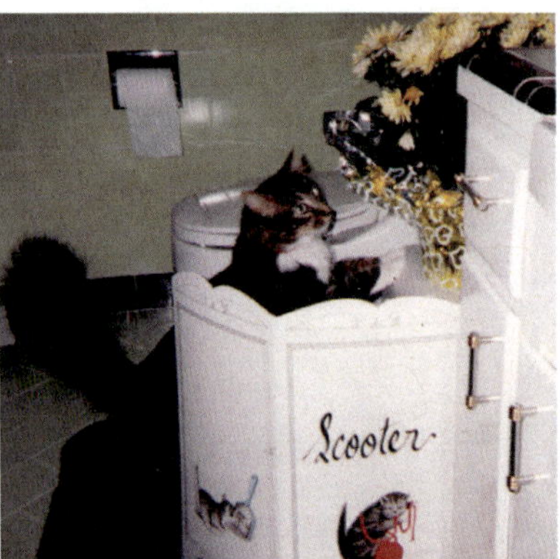

AUTHENTIC: TO BE OR NOT TO BE? THAT IS THE QUESTION.

Authentic: genuine, original, real, actual.
Made or done in the traditional or original way.
Based on fact: accurate or reliable. Dependable, trustworthy and honest.

There you have it. The definition of authentic straight from the dictionary. How is that for an overwhelming, but honorable goal?

As children we are taught to mind our manners, be seen and not heard, respect our elders and more. How in the world can you just be yourself when every second you are making sure that you are following your lessons? We learn early on that the way to get by is to follow those rules and you will have pats on the head, an extra cookie and know that you are loved. Believe that and I have a bridge I want to sell you.

Generationally, parenting was guided by things like "Spare the rod, spoil the child." It wasn't important for us to be ourselves, we had to please our family.

My mother standing with a belt in her hand would say, "You will thank me someday. This is character building," as she glared at us with rage. I became quite a character but never was grateful!

Unfortunately, I will never know if she came from a situation where child abuse was the norm or that she was so unhappy in her life that she took out her misery on her children. Interestingly enough, I kept watching but never saw her show remorse or apologize for anything.

You have been reading my story and you have stuck with me so far. You know that I spent my childhood through my adult years pleasing those around me, hiding in the now very worn-out green velvet pea pod just following what I sensed was the safest way to act in any given situation.

I do think that my theatrical years taught me well how to "fake it 'til you make it." I developed a keen sense of humor and could make a joke or self-deprecate like the best of comedians. Imagine what a life I would have had if I had become a stand-up comedian. That would be AUTHENTIC and a good hearty laugh. Isn't it true that clowns are basically very sad?

Instead, I tucked away my dreams and made sure that everyone else had their dreams, goals and desires fulfilled. I appeared to be independent, self-sustained, never had a worry in the world and could respond within seconds to any situation. I tucked away Carol and made sure that she stayed behind the invisible shield. Every time I saw the toothpaste commercial on television and it showed the "invisible shield," I recognized it instantly as a wall that I possessed and not around my teeth.

My dreams and hopes were quickly dashed by family expectations. I left Theater Arts classes at college and was brought back from Los Angeles by my father. My desire to take over my father's pharmacies (not for girls), my activist self and desire to study law was just a battle I couldn't win. I let my parents bring me home from the ballet company and put me to work at the Jewish Community Center, across from my father's pharmacy. He would drive me to work and bring me home. When home, my mother had me doing household chores and waiting on her.

I knew that there was only one escape for me and that was to marry. As fate will have it, as you read in an earlier chapter, Eugene Sosnick appeared one evening at the Jewish Center, dropped his gym bag on the counter and the answer to pleasing my family had arrived. It wasn't about falling in love, it was about the right family. Eugene was handsome, an all-star basketball player in college and buddies with my cousin, Wally. He was the third, and extremely spoiled third son of Melvin and Celia. There were two daughters-in-law before me so I quickly learned the drill. Eugene was, within months, delegated to our branch of the business in Sacramento and that is the beginning of the next nine years of my life without an authentic bone in my body. It was a game of following the leader and not making trouble.

By a stroke of good fortune, I was blessed with two wonderful babies. I was never a maternal person, preferring to not babysit, or even hold anyone's baby. I just knew the demands. As much as I was in love with my brother, Stephen, when he came home from the hospital, I was terrified when it was my role as a mom.

Eugene was married before and had a son, David. As you recall, Eugene would take me to Stockton with him for his visit with his son, drop me on a street corner while he went to pick up David. Don't you think that was enough of a red flag for me to run, not pass go, collect two hundred dollars and get away from this thoughtless man? Oh no, I was following expectations. Remember, nothing authentic about me!

Nine years later, broken, depressed, lonely and worried for my children, I asked to separate and give Gene time to decide if he wanted a family or not.

He needed a swear box for every time he used an expletive when addressing me. He was rarely home, spent all his time with men friends and spectator sports. I just felt that he was a poor role model for two young sons. I didn't want them to be drinkers, disrespect women and be confused with a bad example. With a heavy heart, I did what you would all expect me to do.

Preparing to leave, I purchased all the same size packing cartons, packed a bit each day and hid the boxes in the closet so Gene would not be upset. Little did I realize the relief he would feel when he could pretend to have a family somewhere but not have to pretend to be an active dad. Before I left, I had his shoes all polished, refreshed his entire wardrobe, put his suits and shirts by color hanging in the closet and left him the convenience of good order.

As a reminder, my parents and Eugene's parents lived one house away from each other in San Francisco's Anzavista neighborhood, isn't that ironic? When I left Sacramento, I stayed with my parents for some months until I could find an appropriate rental. As you recall from a previous chapter, being one house apart you can imagine how that affected any attempt we might have to put our shattered life back together. I could not believe Celia's unkindness. Oh wait, yes, I could!

With the reference to Eugene's father's statement about money in the earlier chapter, it was as if money could buy happiness. It certainly can buy you a good hospital bed but you will still wear the same hospital gown as others, eat the same food and be treated by the same caregivers as all the other patients. How sad that Mr. Sosnick, Marvin and Peter, Eugene's brothers, all died victims of Cancer from smoking and their money could not save them.

As you have read in this memoir, it took seventy-six years to finally reach my authentic self. After an extreme case of exhaustion, therapy and three years, I began to find myself learning the meaning of self-care.

Rather late in life but still time to develop, savor and experience my authenticity.

Continuing to write my story makes my heart sing. I am blessed with healthy friendships, not toxic, and have learned from a dear friend that NO is a complete sentence. I feel things in my soul and get butterflies in my stomach; I can feel emotion. I have taken time to educate and care for myself. I stopped cringing when I looked into the mirror and thought what a fake I was. What started out as such a challenge has great rewards. Each day I grow a little more and see miracles all around me. Yes, love is the answer and also the most authentic emotion of all.

Authentic: genuine, original, real... Carol Loew today!

EPILOGUE

It is Saturday, November 6, 2021, I am sitting at my desk deciding what I want to write to close this memoir of my life so far. I want to satisfy all the questions that I imagine you might have after reading my story. I always wanted to write a book but pushed that project on a back-burner every time I thought about it. I never expected I would write a memoir.

Having written a column for "The Voice," the Jewish Federation quarterly newsletter, while I was serving as Chairman of the Board, it was my first awareness that I could communicate well through the written word. I had several fans that sent a text to share how much they enjoyed my column. That was the first time that I thought seriously about starting to write. Then, my dear friend, Jon Fish, asked me to write, what I thought was five paragraphs, about the Jewish religion for his interfaith Ejournal.

Laughingly, I called Jon and asked, "With a heathen like me, what would you want me to write?"

"Oh," stated Jon, in his loving and warm voice, "write about the Jewish Federation and the Jewish Community Relations Council. Two very important parts of a Jewish Community."

"Thanks, Jon," I answered with much relief. "That I can do. That's around five paragraphs, right?"

"You must not have heard me correctly," he answered. "It is five pages."

With a hearty chuckle, I sat down and wondered what I would say that would take up five pages. It was a piece of cake. I knew what I was writing about, that helped. Before I knew it, I had five pages plus!

And so it began. My neighbor, Sue, suggested I join her in a beginning writing class at Mission Oaks Community Center. Since it was midway in the class, I decided to wait for the new semester and that began September, 2018. There I met another heroine of my story, Kelli Wheeler, our instructor. Young, enthusiastic, kind, welcoming and just the right skill set to be sensitive to neophyte writers telling their own story. As a side note, I purchased a cardboard suitcase to be my writing tool box and it had imprinted on the top "Let the Adventure Begin" and, indeed, it did.

My first anxiety was how to explain the life of a San Francisco Jewish girl with a privileged lifestyle without alienating the entire class by sounding arrogant. After all, wealth can buy things but it can't buy love and authenticity. Sitting without saying a word, I finally decided I had to speak with Kelli and explain my concerns.

"Carol," Kelli said with such kindness, "we love hearing stories of other cultures in our class. That is the joy of sharing stories."

Being aware that there is a solution to every problem, I pondered for days to find that answer. Thus, the stories "Big Grandpa & Little Grandma" and "Little Grandpa & the Wicked Witch of the West" and their arrival at Ellis Island as immigrants in San Francisco with only the hope of success in the Land of Milk and Honey. I had found the solution to begin my history. Kelli had me share the finished story with the class.

What a surprise at our next class when one of my fellow future writers, Linda Curtis, brought a bowl of hummus and a platter of pita bread for the group to enjoy. It made me feel accepted and able to continue with my story.

From there the story began to flow. You have read about "Parenting D-", my siblings, growing up, school days and marriages. What a roller-coaster ride my life has been with scattered challenges and miracles. To be able to capture it on paper and relive my life through my writing is filled with joy, sadness, failure and achievements. When I began this journey, I thought I had nothing good to write about but each chapter has taken me down the path of my life and made me happy to be me.

I have written this manuscript for every child that has not felt loved, woman that has always held second place (as society dictated in my generation), every person that has tried and failed. Remember, you cannot be a success unless you have had the lessons of failure. For things to fall in place, self-care and loving yourself first will unveil the secret of your search.

Now, to update you on my world. I am still living in the large two-story condo that I shared with Harry. Before he passed, he sat me down and instructed me, "When I am gone, get out of this house, it is too big for you alone. In addition to his first recommendation, he underlined on paper, "Stop giving all your money to charity, hang on to your money, do things for yourself." I don't have to tell you how that worked!

While I was offended by his statements, I answered with a bit of a nasty tone in my voice, "You won't be here and you have no right to tell me where to live and what to do with my money. After all, I haven't been using your funds."

That was six years ago so let's move on.

My BFF, Lorraine, has encouraged me to establish what she calls the "Carol Fund" and coaches me on a regular basis to give my charity money to that fund. Lorraine is not only loving, caring, and thoughtful but the honest friend that will tell you that you have spinach in your teeth. She surpasses friendship and is truly my sister of another mother.

My sister, Beverly* and I are the older generation of the clan. Beverly is living in Sacramento at Eskaton, a senior independent facility that closely resembles the cruise ship that never sails. My beloved brother, Stephen, of blessed memory, has been gone seven years and not a day goes by that I don't ache with the loss and feel that a part of my body is missing. How different life would be if he was still with us.

I have become somewhat of a loner. Actually, I think I always had that instinct which is why I worked so hard at my "happiest girl in town" fake behavior. The pandemic stay-at-home was perfect for my transition to an authentic person. I learned to enjoy my home, began the big purge that should be done to avoid bringing-on-the-dumpster-and-chuck-everything-into-it action of emotional children who have no idea what matters and what should be dumped. Having given up most of the volunteer duties that made my life full, it is amazing how free one feels when they have learned the lessons of self needs. I have been home, due to the pandemic, since March 2020. The shelves, drawers and closets still seem overcrowded and much work is still needed. Of course, there is always tomorrow to do it!

Within the next year, my goals are to downsize for ease of maintaining a healthy living environment. Harry's story about being a Holocaust survivor and his life after the Holocaust is my next choice to write. A subject usually ignored when telling the devastation of life being turned upside down as Hitler took over Austria and Harry and his family ended up in Shanghai.

I want to write a humorous book about giving up parenthood once your child is 25 and a full adult. Time to let your children find their way and only give advice when asked. I think I will dig into my comedic self for that one.

To quote an acquaintance of mine, "keep your mouth shut and your handbag open."

My latest revelation is that I have not been a top-notch relationship person. In dealing with my authenticity, I think I have discovered that I was the culprit in the relationship department in many ways. That, too, deserves a reach into my humor gene for an entertaining little book about relationships. Nothing like the story of your life to teach a lesson without a chance to white it out and do-over!

What I know today is that life is good. It doesn't happen without work but, most of all, loving whom and what you are in this life. Always be the best you can possibly be. I realize today that by being authentic, I am happier, and people are gentle and honest. Another dear friend, Elissa, gave me a compliment and a zinger.

With love in her voice, Elissa said, "You know what Carol, I have to tell you that the most wonderful thing about our conversations is that you give me hope. You are certainly not the same person as you were five years ago."

Isn't that just beautiful? Can you imagine that I found a way to say what I wanted to say by talking to others, not at them? How many discussions with family, friends and children have gone in the wrong direction because of my desire to be heard? I couldn't see that I appeared pushy and like a know-it-all.

What an experience this has been. Another miracle waiting to happen. If one person reads this book and learns to self-care I am overjoyed. If it inspires one person to walk down the yellow brick road of their life and write about it, or I can touch one person with a more authentic way to live, my goal has happened. Someone has learned how to live their best life, something that has taken me decades to do.

Writing this memoir has been the most wonderful experience. My heart beats with appreciation for my higher spirit guiding me to learn about myself. The connections are truthful and clear, I have made friends for a lifetime. Stoic and toxic no longer guide me. It is the beauty of the blue sky, gorgeous colors and aroma of living flora, the soft kiss on the nose by a beloved pet. It is gratitude to have a roof over my head and food on the table giving me a happy heart and a perpetual smile on my face. I am truly blessed.

*Beverly passed away January 24, 2022

*"A woman who writes has power,
and a woman with power is feared."*

Gloria Anzalsua

CAROL's TOP TEN LIST

1) If you try to please everyone, no one is happy
If you please yourself first, in the trickle down, everyone is happy

.

2) Always remember, hate is not the opposite of love the opposite of love is fear; think about it and see if there isn't something that you fear.

3) Parenting should be dedicated for twenty-five years, then your children should be your acquaintances.

4) Success can not be attained until you have learned to handle failure and humility. Then you are a true success at what you do.

5) Write your story. You will be surprised by the joy that you experience. Without seeing it as a manuscript, you would not appreciate the journey.

6) Keep your friends close and your enemies closer. you will find that you don't have enemies any longer.

7) When you are being nice, you always hope for a connection and can be disappointed. When you are being kind, you have no expectation and a full happy heart.

8) The miracles are really all around you. Don't be afraid to look for them. Once you find the first one, watch what happens.

9) Life is short. Make good use of the time but remember to stop for a hot fudge sundae or world's greatest chocolate chip cookie.

.

10) And never forget: no is a complete sentence.

ACKNOWLEDGMENTS: POCKETFUL OF MIRACLES

If you happen to be a follower of the "Course in Miracles" you have discovered that it is a very complicated read. Part basic sense and much more, but so complex that you stop in the middle and ponder. The biggest lesson is that miracles are all around us if you concentrate and look for them. Oh, you don't believe it. Trust me, they are everywhere but we are never taught to look for them. How I wish that I knew what was available sooner or, perhaps, in the right time and place to understand what I was seeing.

As long as we are talking about miracles, I find it time to honor and express my appreciation for the miracles that have passed through my life. People, pets and philanthropy have taught me the most about life and how to live it. Let's begin with Carol's miracles.

I am very grateful to my dear parents that gave me life. Beverly and Stephen, my sister and brother (of blessed memory), for teaching me how to share, fight and make up. Sometimes not liking each other very much but always loving each other.

My sons, Craig and Joel, have taught me more about life than I ever expected to learn. Since there are no classes on parenting, I did it by hit and miss. Have I been the "Mother of a Lifetime," Hardly. Did I raise two fine men, yes, but not because of anything I did. They are independent, self- sufficient and many times distanced from me. I imagine they have several issues being raised by a single mother and an absentee father. However, it was the way it was and I am proud of the men that they are today. As with all children, there are days when I wonder what I did wrong but then I swell with pride when they walk into my home or I walk down the street with them. My chickens coming home to roost is my happy time. My children have helped me to grow up and they are a true blessing (most of the time).

Christine, my daughter of another mother, loyal, honest, visible and never losing touch as the years have passed; each conversation, no matter the distance, was like picking up as though we spoke every day. She was my constant blessing.

Every greeting card, embroidered sampler and book about friendship would not be enough words for my dear friend, Lorraine. If you are truly blessed, you will have your own Lorraine in your life. She is the friend that has no limitations to what she will do for you. She asks for nothing, shows up when you need her and she will usually be bearing a pot of Chicken Soup. Through tears and laughter, life and death, sickness and health, shopping or eating, I must have done something very wonderful to have this woman by my side. Now that is a miracle.

Sue Henderson, my dear neighbor, was a mere acquaintance until she saved my life. We were always cordial, waved coming and going, but simply good neighbors. Until, I hit a wall and then Sue became my special angel.

Our friendship speaks to the fact that our higher spirit always leads us to where we need to be. On a very difficult Sunday when I thought my anxiety would not allow me to make it through the day, I called my doctor, pharmacist, pharmacist friend and more and no answer anywhere. Remembering that Sue was a therapist, I called her. Apologizing first, I explained my situation and need for help. She was by my side with comfort and understanding practically before I hung up the telephone. She stayed with me, recommended her office mate whose practice was Post Traumatic Stress Syndrome. That is how Nancy came into my life. As though Sue had not helped enough, she encouraged me to take a writing class with her and this memoir is the result of her introducing me to the art of writing. Sue has been and remains to this day my special angel.

If all my blessings so far were not enough, the greatest gift was joining the most caring, sensitive, smart and clever participants in our writing group. Discovery, joy, friendship and common goals brought us together in a way that binds us forever. It could not happen without the guidance of our leader, Kelli. Her knowledge, encouragement and kindness was the impetus for wanting to do our best. However, the sharing of lives, insight into another person's memories is eye opening. When you think you are alone and frightened, questioning your decisions, never sure, you think you are alone in the world. Being exposed to the open hearts of other memoir storytellers is inspiring. Our small group has shared humor, grief, confidential stories and we have been open to show our hearts, our realities and our souls. What an experience and it could not have come at a better time. Gratitude fills my heart space every time I sit down to write and open a Zoom (pandemic rules) to meet with Kelli and my class.

Those are the people, now let me share another precious gift, my pets.

I know, they take too much time, you can't travel like you want if you have them, they are an extra responsibility and more. Wow, if pets are not your thing, you are missing the most unconditional love experience of a lifetime. Just their presence brings a calm and peace that can carry you through the toughest of times.

From my teenage years to this very day, I have had the most amazing, smart and companionable pets ever. It is as though I am blessed to be able to raise the most gentle, kind and loving of G_d's furry babies. From Tour Jete, my first poodle to Sir Bentley, now my boy for just a few weeks, there has been a constant flow of extraordinary poodles. The last two, Mocha, a brown toy and Chelsea, a salt and pepper toy never met a stranger and charmed everyone. Chelsea was easily recognizable as she always walked with a toy in her mouth. Sir Bentley or as I like to call him Ben, is a handsome large miniature, would you believe I was looking for a teacup toy girl, but Chelsea must have decided that I needed to have Bentley and arranged for me to find him. I was really in the right place at the right time to give Ben a forever home and me a new reason to fall in love.

Chelsea returns to me daily as the most beautiful yellow butterfly. She visits me first and I watch her as she flies from home to home checking everyone out. She reminds me every day of the miracles that surround us all the time if we only watch for them and embrace them when we see them. She taught me acceptance of all, kindness, gentility, unconditional devotion and reminded me daily that loving deeply is available in many ways and circumstances. She never ceased to teach me lessons that would make my heart happy and put a smile on my face.

To those I may have forgotten that encouraged, pushed and prodded to keep me on track, my love and thanks. You know who you are!

I do believe that my pocketful is flowing over. I could never be where I am today without my miracles.

Made in the USA
Middletown, DE
22 December 2023